THE CHILD AND THE INSTITUTION

A Study of Deprivation and Recovery

It has long been believed that children who must spend much of their lives in institutions inevitably develop personality deficiencies that make them liabilities to society. This book represents the first portion of a longitudinal study of the children of the Neil McNeil Home from infancy into adulthood. The study was begun in 1957 with a twofold purpose: first, to provide a therapeutic environment for children who had already suffered mental and emotional damage from an institutional milieu; and second, to devise methods of institutional care that would conduce to the normal development of children deprived of the usual supports of family relationships. The case histories presented here are interesting documents in themselves, but the book is more than a study of individual cases. It presents a detailed description of the process of creating in a child-care institution something of the atmosphere of a normal home. The conclusions reached depart in significant ways from former studies of institutionalized children, and will be of great importance and usefulness both to those who work professionally with children and to those concerned with the social future of children raised outside the family unit. The book was sponsored by the Institute of Child Study, University of Toronto.

BETTY FLINT, Assistant Professor of Child Study in the Institute of Child Study, University of Toronto, has had practical experience as a supervisor of playgrounds and in the operation of day camps and a nursery school. She has lectured in child development and psychology at Ryerson Polytechnical Institute, and has served as Clinical Psychologist for the Children's Aid Society of Metropolitan Toronto, Consultant to the Neil McNeil Infants' Home during the rehabilitation period described herein, and supervisor of the Infant section of the Research Department, Institute of Child Study. She is the author of *The Security of Infants,* published by the University of Toronto Press.

THE CHILD
AND THE
INSTITUTION

A Study
of Deprivation
and Recovery

Betty Margaret Flint

UNIVERSITY OF TORONTO PRESS

© *University of Toronto Press 1966*

Reprinted 2017

ISBN 978-1-4875-9870-9 (paper)

Foreword

THE PRECISE and detailed manner in which Professor Flint has documented the happenings at Neil McNeil Infants' Home reflects the intensive interest and participation of the Institute of Child Study in the problems of institutional care. *The Child and the Institution* is a concise record of the remedial measures that were effected subsequent to 1957 to rehabilitate the children in the care of the Home. If there are causes and effects to be scientifically researched in a study of maternal deprivation of infants, then, certainly, the effects are vividly portrayed in this book.

I cannot help but remind the reader that the effectiveness of the programme was the responsibility of Miss Mary Kilgour, whose direction and co-ordination of the activities of many interested persons resulted in the achievements recorded here.

The Catholic Children's Aid Society of Metropolitan Toronto is indebted to Professor Flint for her documentation of an experiment that may well be of tremendous assistance to those involved in child care.

W. WARD MARKLE
Executive Director
Catholic Children's Aid Society

August 31, 1965

Acknowledgments

THIS PROJECT developed from the joint concerns of two separate institutions with different aims and orientations, but with a common concern for the welfare of children. The Catholic Children's Aid Society of Metropolitan Toronto, beset by the practical problem of placing young children for adoption, was seeking ways to relieve the effects of deprivation due to institutional care. The Institute of Child Study of the University of Toronto was academically interested in understanding the specific causes and effects of deprivation in early childhood, and in using this information for the benefit of other children. The co-operative effort which arose from the blending of these practical and academic considerations led to a unique and fruitful outcome.

As the project took shape, many people became touched with the idea that rehabilitation was possible. Enthusiasm was unbounded. So intensely did people identify with the children and become concerned with their progress that the term "our children" was unconsciously used. What "we" did in terms of the programme was discussed by people who had even a minimal role in the total plan.

It is impossible to name all the people whose enthusiasm and dedication contributed to the ultimate success of the rehabilitation programme. Mr. Ward Markle, Chairman of the Board and later Executive Director of the Catholic Children's Aid Society, gave wholehearted support to the recommendations for programme changes and to the steps necessary to carry them out. Professor Dorothy Millichamp gave invaluable assistance to the initial planning of the treatment centre. Mary Kilgour, R.N., DIP. C.S., undertook the monumental task of making the plan a reality. Under her astute direction a staff developed whose enthusiasm and dedication were truly remarkable. Volunteer "mothers," and later adoptive and foster mothers, played a unique role without which all progress in rehabilitation would have ended.

Further acknowledgment is made to the Ontario Mental Health Foundation, Research Grant #18; to the Laidlaw Foundation; to the National Mental Health Grant, Project 605-5-353: Infant Security Studies; and to the W. E. Blatz Memorial Fund for the various kinds of support they have given to this study.

B.M.F.

Contents

Introduction

WHEN THIS STUDY BEGAN in 1957, there was widespread interest in the phenomenon of "maternal deprivation," a term broadly used to describe a state resulting from the early separation of a young child from his mother. Three sorts of separation were recognized: a permanently disrupted mother-child relationship, such as would have been experienced by children living in institutions; a discontinuous relationship which results from a broken home or a series of foster homes and changing mothers; and a relationship characterized by inconsistent and erratic mothering, such as might result if the mother were ill or neurotic. The symptoms arising from these experiences had a common syndrome recognizable not only in the months and years immediately following deprivation, but also in later life, particularly during adolescence. Prognosis for recovery from the effects of deprivation was poor. Permanent damage to emotional well-being usually ensued.

Since 1957 a great variety of studies have confirmed the kinds of personality deficiencies resulting from maternal deprivation. The deficiencies are most clearly evident in children reared in institutions during their early years. They appear in early infancy and perpetuate themselves throughout the person's life. An inability to form relationships with adults or contemporaries, inadequate intellectual function, apathy and indifference to one's world, and poor physical stamina are some of the most obvious symptoms. The behaviour of such children precludes successful adjustment to foster or adoptive homes and results in permanent residence either in a series of institutions through the child's growing years or in a variety of foster homes tried one after another in a vain attempt to find a congenial one where the child could be accepted by foster parents.

Such experiences produce children to whom family or community values are meaningless and who could broadly be described as psychopathic personalities. From a personal point of view, they are doomed to a life remote from relationships with other people. Furthermore, many of them become delinquent and spend a lifetime in and out of penal training institutions or mental institutions. Such people are the causes of unhappiness both to themselves and to the victims of their delinquent acts. In addition, an enormous expense is carried by the community for their special care.

Because the necessity of caring for young children in institutions is always with us, any studies which might reveal ways of improving institutional care to foster both mental and physical health would be of tremendous value to any community, and to child welfare agencies in particular. This particular study has revealed some effective channels of treatment and has pointed the way for improved institutional care. All the answers have not been found, and the full impact of the adequacy of treatment will be revealed only as we continue to study this group of children through the years. But enough has been discovered to merit the attention of anyone interested in improving the lives of deprived children living in and out of institutions.

PART ONE • THE BEGINNING

1

Research

IS THE DEVELOPMENT of children reared in an institution so distorted as to cause permanent damage? Some experts think so. Some are not sure. No proof yet exists, although a great deal of the published evidence points to this conclusion. This book is an account of a group of children living in the Neil McNeil Home, an institution caring for infants and young children under the administration of the Catholic Children's Aid Society of Metropolitan Toronto. Although each institution has unique characteristics, similar deficiencies in living arrangements exist in all, and the behaviour of the children described here is similar to that of children reared in institutions in widespread parts of the world. The milieu of an institution creates common distortions in behaviour and in affective life which can be isolated and described with remarkable similarity wherever the institution may exist.

The study presented here started as a research project and developed into an experiment in human living which attempted to rehabilitate those youngsters who had lived their first months and years under conditions of emotional deprivation. As far as we know, this study is unique in recording observations of infants first in their deprived state, then during a period of treatment, and finally in foster and adoptive homes. Close contact is still being maintained with each child in his new home and community, and the adequacy and comfort of his adjustment are carefully watched. By this method we hoped to assess the degree to which deprivation can be relieved, and make some judgement regarding the potential of deprived children to respond to a benign environment and become productive and happy citizens.

Our study had started under a unique combination of circumstances which encouraged us to grasp the opportunity to study deprived children in a typical institution. The Neil McNeil Home was the only

institution of its kind remaining in Toronto (18), devoted entirely to
the care of infants and pre-school children. The Catholic Children's
Aid Society, which was responsible for the care and ultimate future
of the children, was seeking a change, hoping that better care at this
age would mean a more optimistic future than had been the lot of
the hundreds of children who had passed through its doors and those
of many like institutions in the past. A child-study specialist was
available who knew the organization and some of the children, and
a great variety of community sources were open for her use (19). In
addition, sufficient interest from lay people in the community had
resulted in a grant of money to initiate an improved child-centred
programme. The opportunity not only to introduce the change, but
to provide the treatment and to assess the results, was too good to
lose. Surely we could obtain valuable information about the welfare
of these children, information which in turn would enrich the general
fund of knowledge about institutionalized children.

Starting from our knowledge of the needs of normal children and
our ability to provide for them, we initiated treatment by aiming for
a "model" environment. Broadly, treatment consisted of environmental
adaptation which would guide each child's development in the direction of normal behaviour. The children's response to these modifica-
tions and their capacity to meet environmental expectations were
assessed from time to time. The response of the total group was
evaluated first, and then each child's reaction was studied. This assessment acted as a guide to the next modification in the programme in
the direction of normal living. The process was continued until each
child showed sufficient signs of adequacy (or mental health) to be
ready for foster or adoptive placement. The goal was that the treatment programme should initiate the process of normal development
and that foster and adoptive placement should integrate and confirm it.

The study began in 1957 when we were seeking a group of children
on which to test the validity of the Infant Security Scale, a measure
developed for the purpose of assessing mental health in young children
up to two years of age. My early research on young children had led
to the conclusion that mental health is influenced from infancy. The
elaboration of the "infant security theory" underlies the Infant Security
Scale (18). Prior to 1957, the scale had been tried on several groups
of children, mainly those who were being reared in homes within the
framework of a family. Literature on maternal deprivation and my
own observations of children being reared in institutions made it

evident that a group of institutionalized infants would differ widely from any previous groups we had chosen for observation.

At this time, Miss Mary Kilgour, a registered nurse completing study for her diploma at the University of Toronto's Institute of Child Study, was ready to work on the research project with me. Her earlier experiences with young children, particularly infants, provided good background knowledge for a project to measure the mental health of institutionalized babies. We therefore approached the officials of the Neil McNeil Home, which had been operating for many years in Toronto, and had provided shelter for children who awaited adoption or whose homes had been temporarily broken up. We knew that it was seriously overcrowded, at that time housing eighty-five children, although it was really adequate for only fifty. We also knew that it had been established to care for very young children, but, that as a constant trickle of newly born babies needing shelter continued to swell its population, while a shortage of foster and adoptive homes blocked their discharge, many of the children had grown well beyond infancy and some were as old as three and a half years. In view of this, we were well aware that the programme of the home could not possibly meet many of the children's needs. The Catholic Children's Aid Society was eager to co-operate with our project, provided that we report some of our findings to them. Miss Kilgour proceeded with her research, selecting sixteen children and observing each of them one day each month for five months. When the collection of data was completed, we analysed it clinically and (also) derived mental health scores. As we had anticipated, our results showed that on the whole these children compared very unfavourably with a similar group of children reared in their own homes. One alarming indication was that every child showed a decrease in security scores over the five-month observation period. A comparison in the scores of the youngest and oldest children showed that the decrease in the scores grew more marked the longer institutional care was prolonged. It appeared to be certain that institutional care had a detrimental effect on mental health, and our conclusions corroborated the published results of other research workers interested in the same phenomenon.

However, one piece of evidence differed from research results being reported at the time these studies were undertaken. Most of the literature on deprived infants had stated that all children reared in institutions suffered permanent damage to their mental health (11). Our results (18) made us question this depressing conclusion. There were marked differences among children of approximately the same age who had had the same length of institutional experience. Furthermore, although all scores tended to move progressively down, each child showed his own unique pattern. This led us to believe that some children had more emotional stamina than others, enabling them to sustain their feeling of well-being even though all were living in the same cold and barren environment. Our observations, coupled with our intuitive feeling about the children as we worked with them, made us feel hopeful that institutional care need not be permanently damaging for all children. The apparent resilience of some children indicated they might have a capacity to respond to psychological treatment which could ultimately lead to their rehabilitation (18). We anticipated that some of them could gradually learn to trust adults and other children and could form normal relationships with them, eventually making an adequate adjustment to the community and becoming useful and happy citizens. We feared, however, that without treatment these children were doomed to the bleak and lonely future faced by many former residents of institutions in the past.

We reported our findings, impressions, and conclusions to the Catholic Children's Aid Society. At that time the care of institutionalized children was becoming a serious administrative and community problem for the Society. Because the behaviour of the children in the McNeil Home had been so distorted, they could not successfully go from the institution to either a foster or adoptive home, and therefore would remain a liability to themselves and the community for the rest of their lives. They would probably move from one institution to another until they were considered legally old enough to take care of themselves. The few placements that had been tried at sporadic intervals had consistently failed; it would be only a rare family that would have the understanding and patience to live with such youngsters. The rewards of caring for them were almost nil. The problem was not only a community problem, but also a human one, bringing misery to the children who had no choice but to remain in custodial care. The fact was that the longer the children remained in the institution, the more remote from normal living they became. Although the immediate problem was specific to the McNeil Home, the difficulties could be generalized to any agency or institution caring for young children.

When our findings and conclusions were discussed with the board of the Catholic Children's Aid Society, it was most eager to take whatever measures were possible to alleviate the situation. We felt confident that we could offer some suggestions which might help the

Society to treat these children in such a way that they could adjust to a normal life. The Society requested that some members of the staff of the University of Toronto's Institute of Child Study undertake a programme to aid the rehabilitation of the youngsters in the McNeil Home. Here was an opportunity to test our judgement that at least some of them could be helped. Could we, using our knowledge and practical skills, bring about at least partial recovery of mental health? We accepted the challenge, and we felt we must take it up as a vital human problem, as well as a research project.

2

Help through Play

NOW THAT the opportunity for a study was here, we were faced with the question of what could be done. It was evident that the children's greatest need was for a satisfying emotional milieu, something almost impossible to achieve within the Neil McNeil Home as it was then organized. However, it was possible to provide play equipment for those children who might be mentally able to respond to it: who might show signs of interest when stimulated, and who could emerge a little from their self-preoccupation.

Our second approach was connected with adult-child relationships. It was evident that the children had had only superficial relationships with the adults in the McNeil Home. Indeed, many seemed to have given up any attempt to initiate contacts at all. We wondered if some better kind of relationship might be formed with children by adults who were teaching them how to use play materials and demonstrating that satisfactions could be had in this way.

We therefore recommended that toys and play equipment be obtained for a playroom somewhat like that of a regular nursery-school, but adapted to the children's obvious immaturity. We also recommended that the playroom be supervised by two adults trained in psychology and having sufficient skill to stimulate the children on the level best suited to them. The staff should also recognize the necessity of forming a close relationship with the child, a relationship we considered a prerequisite to adequate performance with the play materials. They should recognize that play was a natural way for a child to express himself. We hoped that the self-confidence gained by a child who had been encouraged in the use of toys would lead him to express some aspect of his personality. In addition, each child might gain confidence in the knowledge that there was at least one adult in his world who could be relied on to treat him as an individual.

Our recommendations resulted in the appointment of two highly trained and experienced people to supervise and equip the playroom. Miss Mary Kilgour, who had carried out our original study and since then had received her diploma in Child study, was appointed for two and a half days weekly. Her knowledge of the institution and of children was of immeasurable help in organizing a playroom. Her assistant, Miss Lila Goldenberg, a nursery school teacher, was to work four half-days a week. Both were trained to keep systematic records of the children's activity, and a plan to evaluate the children's progress was mapped out before the project got under way. This plan and the record-taking were supervised by some of the research staff at the Institute of Child Study, Professor Millichamp and myself acting as advisers.

Miss Kilgour and her assistant bought the materials and play equipment and organized two attractive basement playrooms for the children. Small tables and chairs, cupboards for toys, a doll centre, a piano, books, a variety of plants and live animals (fish, turtles, kitten, etc.), records, dishes, provisions for water play, puzzles, cars, trucks, and boats were provided. One of the main considerations was the need to acquaint the children, who had seen nothing beyond the walls of the institution, with some of the aspects of normal living. A mirror in the doll centre provided a source of satisfaction and bewilderment, for these children had never seen themselves before.

We recognized that conditions for the project were far from ideal. Our first study (18) had indicated that any work towards improved mental health has the highest chance of success if it is applied to infants under nine months of age, since after that time the detrimental effects of the institution on personality appear to grow steadily worse. However, because the money available for the project was limited, we could only select children from a limited age group (22 months to 3 years), and because of the considerable immaturity of the children, we were only able to work with a very small number. Therefore, nine children were chosen who seemed typical of the group, and they were regarded as an experimental group, permitting us to evaluate how much or how little such a play programme could contribute to their recovery. We were touching only a small segment of their lives, but we had to be content working in relative isolation from their everyday experiences.

The playroom was open for two hours each afternoon for approximately four and a half months. We planned to introduce the children gradually to the playroom programme over a period of some weeks, as it was evident that very few could be supervised at once in the initial stages, owing to their lack of inner resources. Our naive expectation was that eventually all nine children could be brought to the enjoyment of something resembling a regular nursery school playroom.

At the beginning the children were brought to the playroom one at a time by the supervisor. It was necessary to hold their hands and to take them to the toys and show them exactly what could be done with each one. The children were consistently bewildered and erratic. They were totally lacking in interest and could not even manipulate the toys when one was handed to them. They could not, or would not, follow the directions of the adult, and had to be physically helped to do everything. If two children were taken to a playroom together, even if separately supervised by the two staff members, their lack both of control of themselves and of confidence in adults resulted in highly excited, distractible behaviour. Teaching the use of toys was almost impossible. If requested by the adult to *choose* a toy, they were thrown into complete confusion. Making choices was much too complex a form of behaviour for them. When they were directed to do anything, they either balked in fear or stood passively staring at the adult. Their social skills with each other were almost non-existent: no child was able to cope with more than one other child in the playroom. Not only were they distracted by each other, they had not even rudimentary skills in playing together. Each child coming to the playroom seemed at an emotional extreme, either frightened and overly excited or dull and apathetic towards the whole new situation.

After the first week it was obvious that we could not establish anything like a nursery school playroom in which the children could be expected to settle happily to play under the direction of an adult. We had to modify our plan, since it was apparent that the children could be expected to respond only to some highly individual aspect of play, directed by one adult. For this reason the children were taken one at a time to the playroom and each in turn given the full attention of a supervisor. After the first couple of weeks they could settle for ten to fifteen minutes if constantly supported and encouraged by the adult. Beyond this time they could make no further effort and were reduced to hectic and totally disorganized behaviour. Then they were taken from the playroom back to the nursery. Each child was treated differently, according to the supervisor's evaluation of his emotional state and his probable response.

By the end of the first month, it had been possible to introduce only six of the nine children to the playroom experience. Instead of the anticipated group of eight or nine children playing together at the same time, only three children could be permitted together if chaos was to be avoided. By the end of four and one-half months, only five children could play together constructively for a short time, under the carefully thought out and highly controlled direction of both supervisors. At no time did a group pattern evolve resembling those found in nursery school playrooms.

A recognition of the children's limitations when playing in groups, and an examination of daily records of their response to the play programme, gave us valuable diagnostic tools for estimating the degree of therapy probably necessary to bring about any real improvement in their mental health. Although the response was meagre, varying degrees of improvement could be noted in the play habits of most of the children. Six of the nine children became capable of following their individual play interest for a short while, even with a few other children in the room. We judged that these six showed slight signs of improved mental health.

We had hoped to instil in the children some degree of confidence in adults. In the nursery units, their attitude toward adults had been impersonal and vague. The people taking care of them seemed no more important to them than the furniture, and the children regarded the playroom supervisors in the same way. It therefore was a long while before they paid any attention to these new adults, and longer yet before they regarded them as beneficient. The six children who first responded to the atmosphere of the playroom began showing signs of dependence by looking to the supervisor for attention and by accepting help in finding and choosing playthings. Under intense supervision they were gradually able to settle down with a toy for a short period of constructive effort. Their distrust began to subside if all went smoothly. However, any disturbance caused them to return to their earlier behaviour, to withdraw from the play materials and refuse to co-operate with the adults. Despite this, the general tendency was toward the development of some self-confidence during the play sessions. In addition, the supervisors noted an improvement in the children's capacity to communicate. Their speech had been grossly defective at the beginning of the experiment but showed substantial improvement as the sessions progressed. Whereas pushing, pulling, grunting, and gesturing had predominated at first, gradually a willingness to talk to adults appeared, and the children made an effort to communicate verbally with one another.

The three children who showed no progress seemed held back by their inability to establish any relationship with the adults. They remained indifferent and refused any proffered help and direction. Their behaviour was consistent with the behaviour they had shown in the nurseries: highly emotional and unsettled. Their progress in play habit and skills was extremely limited. They gave the impression of being severely disturbed. The one notable response to the play sessions was an improvement in their speech.

None of the nine children seemed to have any capacity or readiness for social activity. Their lack of self-confidence seemed to preclude the possibility of interaction with other children.

Implications

The limited response both to the adults and to the play situation was an indication that qualities essential for mental health were lacking. The caution with which the children put their trust in an adult on whom they should be depending indicated an absence of early first relationships with the people who cared for them. The gross deficiency in speech, followed by a relatively swift improvement during the course of the play sessions, made it apparent that these children had lacked the warm human contacts which are usually expressed in the chatter between adults and young children and serve to build in a child a feeling of self-worth and a picture of himself as a unique individual (18). The fact that in spite of having lived together for a long time in the same setting, these children were unable to enjoy each other, demonstrated that their social growth had either never started or had been seriously distorted. They seemed to see social contacts as threatening rather than rewarding experiences.

It appeared that any rehabilitation of the children's emotional life would take a considerably longer time than we had anticipated, even in our most pessimistic planning. For a play setting to be salutary at all, it must be based upon a solid foundation of personal relationships. Without this, we saw, any learning through stimulation of the intellect by play materials was doomed to failure. Any really effective improvement in mental health would come only through a complete change of programme, a new staff willing to gear the programme to the needs and abilities of the children rather than make the children conform to the system, and a greatly increased personnel to provide direction, care, love, and control. The attitudes of the staff of the McNeil Home at this time were severely damaging to the children's mental health. This group of unresponsive, aimless, inarticulate children had led the staff to resort to harsh, authoritarian handling in their efforts to achieve even minimal conformity to direction. The harsh treatment further disturbed the emotional state of the children, and a vicious circle had been started.

Thus, as far as the actual play experiment was concerned, it probably had little long-term value for the nine children, despite a temporary outlook for the better. Most discouraging was the inability of the children to establish any sort of communication or empathy (form relationships) with adults or other children. However, one hopeful sign was present in this study, as it had been in our first one (18)— each child responded differently to the play situation, reinforcing our earlier conviction that some children had sufficient resilience to respond positively to a salutary environment. We could still surmise that the deprivation experience had not irrevocably damaged everyone. This idea was expressed concretely in the second major report to the board of the Catholic Children's Aid Society. In the report we stated the steps which were essential to improve the mental health of the children and assist their progress toward normal living. Given the circumstances just described, only a total reorganization of the McNeil Home could accomplish anything. Any attempt to "mop up" through minor changes would not be successful.

3

Recommendations to the Board

THE FOLLOWING EXCERPTS from the report submitted to the board of the Catholic Children's Aid Society contain our main recommendations for changes in the programme. We deliberately elaborated what we considered to be essential changes and attempted to give reasons for our suggestions, keeping in mind that the board comprised a variety of people from the community who would not necessarily appreciate the need or the reasons for changes unless our points were emphatically made and included some description of the emotional state of the children and the routine of the home.

The Report

It is obvious that one of the main deficiencies in these children's lives is the lack of any close relationship with one or two adults. Present knowledge indicates to us that some kind of close emotional relationship with an adult is essential for the well-being of young children. Only through a close tie of this nature can young children develop in themselves any assurance that they too are capable of feeling any warmth or satisfaction in relationships with other people.

It is further obvious that children who have lived in institutions for any length of time are greatly lacking in any desire to put forth effort to make their own lives satisfactory. They play little with toys; attempt to do nothing for themselves, although of an age when they should be capable of this; and many of them do not even make any overtures to people—one of the normal sources of satisfaction to young children.

The third fact which stands out strongly is that these children have little if any self-control. There is no direction to their activity and no attempt to control their emotions. It is true that they show a submissive response to strongly authoritarian direction, but without this they have no inner strength to control their own very limited experiences.

From an administrative point of view, it has appeared feasible that some kind of play programme might be helpful in the enrichment of these children's lives. It was thought possible that play could supply some of their needs, the most obvious of which would be that of introducing them to broader life experiences. It is well known that through the use of play materials young children can develop interest in their environment and a feeling of self-confidence. Such experiences as learning to sit and look at books could give them some insight into aspects of life of which they were unaware. Toys, such as those used in doll centres—water, dolls, beds, dishes, clothing, and so on—could open a new world of experiences. Furthermore, a play programme could introduce a sense of orderliness into their lives. The mere routine of a playroom involving taking a toy off a shelf and replacing it, the firm control and direction of an interested adult, the feeling of self-satisfaction which comes to a child from producing something from his own efforts in the playroom, could possibly introduce a feeling to a child that, at least in some ways, his world was dependable. This, in turn, would foster mental health.

However, owing to the lack of development in these children, such benefits are beyond achievement. Sweeping changes are essential.

Observation of the situation in the institution points up inadequacies in the experience of the children there, inadequacies which would limit them and prevent them from making a normal adjustment to life. The general organization of the institution makes it almost impossible to meet the psychological needs of the children. Each child is generally confined to one nursery and one outdoor experience each day in the garden. This allows him neither to change his living quarters nor to improve his ability to understand the sequence of time. Nothing is new, nothing is different, therefore nothing is memorable. Life is dull and plodding; an interminable sequence of sameness over and over again. There is no adequate programme of toilet training for any of the children. There is no attempt to catch each child at his stage of readiness. Every child is treated the same. At a certain age, he is placed upon a pot and there is expected to stay until he has achieved success. When he becomes restless, as he naturally will, it is sometimes felt necessary to tie him to the bed in order to keep him sitting there. Prolonged sitting on the pot is causing some prolapsed rectums. The eating habits of the children are also very poor. Here again every child is treated exactly the same. Little opportunity is given for each child to eat at his own pace, and no variety is offered as the children get older. Nor do the children have adequate opportunity to feed themselves, thereby becoming interested in helping themselves.

Although some attempts have been made to improve the living arrangements, the children still spend a great deal more time in bed than is good for them. Their afternoon sleep period begins very late; evidently it is geared to the needs of the nursing staff rather than those of the children. There is a great lack of play equipment. In fact, whatever equipment is available seems completely inadequate, and there is no opportunity for children to really learn how to use it. There has been some progress made in the direction of stimulating the children with little stories and some play material, but this is still greatly below any adequate standard for such a group. The children derive almost no satisfaction from their contacts with each other and they seem to see each other merely as other objects in the environment. No meaningful social inter-action takes places among them. While in their nursery wards, they tend to push, scream, and scramble over one another, and generally behave like undisciplined and unsupervised animals.

At present, there can be no attempt to give special supervision to very difficult children or ones with obvious problems. Those children who need special attention are usually isolated from the rest of the group and rather than getting more attention, are, in effect, neglected and left unattended. Those who are overly aggressive are left quite frequently unsupervised with the rest of the children and constantly create turmoil and fighting. The lack of supervisory staff for the children, particularly in the afternoon period, is a serious threat to their physical safety.

The most serious deficiency of the total programme is the lack of awareness that each child is an individual. No child has any belongings of his own, nor has he any toys of his own. The children are herded in groups from one place to another and no opportunity arises for them to be treated as individuals. Individual treatment is, of course, essential for a child to grow into a socially sensitive person.

With these general inadequacies of the present situation in mind, one can see it is impossible to improve the experiences of these children under existing conditions. An evaluation of the experimental play programme indicates that it had a very limited use. It certainly could not improve the total situation, and it could only touch a few children's lives in a very superficial way.

Observations recorded when the experiment was over indicated that those children who had had the play experiences were more aggressive with the total group, were more interested in play material, and seemed better able to amuse themselves than the rest of the group. Further, there did seem to be some kind of social inter-action among a few of the children who had had the playroom experience. This, of course, would lead us to expect that should any play programme be started on a broad scale without a complete change in programme, the total situation might further deteriorate. The children who would have the play experience would become more and more difficult to live with, and would be impossible to cope with from the point of view of the staff in charge.

The present situation already is a most difficult one for the staff. They become confused and irritated by the many frustrations which come from the screaming children around them. The children's helplessness and lack of responsibility make it very difficult for the staff to maintain an even frame of mind. Should the children become more interested in doing things in a self-directed way, should they become less amenable to a highly authoritarian system of discipline, they would indeed add to the present troubles rather than alleviate them. The present rough handling and shouting which seem to be necessary from the staff would, unfortunately, probably be increased.

It is obvious that the present play programme is attempting to undo damage which started when the children were very much younger. It is therefore evident that any programme providing increased stimulation, individual attention, and broadened experiences should start in early infancy. The conditions which are holding the children back now could be eliminated should such a programme be instituted in the early months of their lives.

The routine care in the institution is fairly good. It is highly organized in some aspects and may be adequate for infants. However, without personalized care children will fail to grow as individuals. Therefore it will be necessary that some change in attitude take place among the staff members who care for the children. It is essential that they have in mind that they are working with individual human beings. Without this, the children's human development will fail to take place. They need much more talking to, more cuddling, broader experiences. They need things which belong to them, such as their own toys, shoes, and clothes. They need one or two persons to whom they can become attached and with whom they will be completely familiar. These persons will recognize their individual idiosyncrasies. For example, they will be able to comprehend when the children start to say words and will be able to reflect back to them what they think is meant by these words. Only in this way can young children learn to grow in the ways expected of them in this culture.

Therefore, the primary change in programme really should take place at the infant level. Only a fundamental change can prepare the children for any continuing programme which might be started at the pre-school level, such as a nursery school.

The second change required in the present setting is to provide therapy for the older children who have already experienced such limited contact with people and with the world. Therapy of this sort will require a person or persons specially trained in meeting the individual needs of each child, even in a very minute way. It will further need a supervisory staff trained in the recognition of psychological needs and a nursing staff prepared to learn and to follow along with a revised programme.

The first period of a year or so after these changes take place will be most difficult, partly because the children will be needing and responding to special care and will, therefore, be more difficult, and partly because a staff in training will be unable to see fully why changes are taking place. Should these two changes come about, it should be possible for these children to grow within normal developmental limits and move forward in a straightforward progression.

There followed specific suggestions regarding change.

Positive Findings

1. All these children have some potentiality for maturing in their personalities and abilities. Some have a great deal of untapped potentiality. In fact, the children need not and should not be in their present hazardous states.

2. A change in their daily living habits would bring about development. Even short periods of play have had an effect.

3. At least some of the children are still capable of forming warm relationships with people—adults and other children—despite the serious lag.

4. A therapeutic play programme is worthwhile and essential as part of a total change in the programme of the Home.

5. Individual therapy is worthwhile and essential for each child at this point, and each child's treatment must be different.

6. Since the deterioration of these children has been progressive from

infancy, it is obvious that to prevent recurrence of the present situation, treatment of the infant group should be revised immediately.

7. While the rehabilitation programme of the present groups of infants and pre-schoolers will be long, difficult, and expensive, it should result (in perhaps two years) in something very different from the present situation. With a group of normally developing children, the staff members will find their work to be natural, interesting, and satisfying. The treatment of the children can then be usual, and while it should remain individualized, it need not be therapeutic.

Suggestions for Total Re-organization

1. The attitude toward the children requires revision: the present mechanical care should be changed to personal concern for each child as an individual; routine should be replaced by an effort to guide and teach; the overall purpose should be the children's growth and *not* the programme.

2. A period of approximately two years should be set up as a "rehabilitation period." Only at the end of such a period, when the children have approached normal status, can a new and consistent "normal" programme come into being.

This period of therapy means facing and solving the difficulties from which the children are suffering, and will necessarily be full of stress for adults. The programme required will not be normal. It requires an unusual programme to treat abnormal children and bring about positive personality changes.

3. As well as being difficult, this programme will be expensive, particularly in terms of staff needs. After this period, however, these needs will decrease.

4. The most important single item for this "rehabilitation period" is staff. The following should be considered:

a. Advisory specialists.

b. Sufficient trained staff to form a demonstration core.

c. Regular nursery staff willing and interested in participating in the rehabilitation programme, and ready to trust their advisers. Each adult will be strategic, and one unwilling person could damage the effort of others.

N.B. Would it be possible to discuss the rehabilitation project with the present staff and give them an opportunity to choose whether they are interested in participating or would prefer to withdraw?

It should be emphasized that the present state of the children is not the fault of the staff. It is the inevitable outcome of unwitting institutional care. We now know that developmental deficiencies occur in any child institution when the hazards are not foreseen.

5. The staff will require:

a. Regular conferences individually and in groups with the specialized personnel.

b. In service training.

c. Possibly an outside discussion group of a professional type.

d. Work with the children along with trained personnel.

6. Programme changes should be slow and flexible, adapted to the changes in the children.

Immediate changes include the following:

a. The routines of eating, sleeping, bathing, dressing, and toilet should change from mechanical adult care to friendly ministering with emphasis on child participation.

b. Unsupervised and purposeless scrambling about in large groups should be replaced by worthwhile activity in small groups.

c. Instead of emotional episodes being ignored or inhibited, they should be treated with solicitude and a solution attempted.

d. Controls should be simple, definite, and kind, and carried out in the same way by all staff members.

e. Each child needs to have signatures of his identity as a person— namely possessions of his own.

f. Most important, each child will need an adult paying particular attention to him. Each staff member could be assigned a certain number of children to whom she gives special attention in little ways here and there throughout the day.

g. With the present pre-school group it will probably be wise to spend more time and effort on those children who respond most quickly to treatment. Unless guarded against, the alternative is likely to occur, that is, that the least able children will receive the most attention. Some children will *not* respond to treatment and this should be accepted without anxiety or blame to the staff. Mental health should be the goal to be achieved wherever possible.

7. The programme for the infants should have priority consideration. Since the infants are closer to normal status, a more adequate programme can be brought in with relative ease.

8. It is important that some type of regular recording be made of both the history of the programme change and the children's progress. Such records are useful:

a. In preventing staff discouragement.

b. In verifying fact versus impression.

c. In providing evidence of progress or failure.

d. In contributing to the knowledge of child care.

Unless record-keeping is definitely assigned, it will be set aside for more immediate urgencies. It should be the responsibility of a staff specialist in child guidance.

PART TWO • PROGRAMME THERAPY

4

Aims, Goals, and Changes

SPURRED by our report and its mounting administrative problem, the board made an intensive effort to find money for a complete rehabilitation programme. The Municipality of Metropolitan Toronto pledged support. Miss Kilgour, who by now was familiar with the children, the McNeil Home, and the Children's Aid Society, was asked to supervise the rehabilitation programme, and some of the staff of the Institute of Child Study were requested to be advisers. Miss Kilgour was admirably suited to guide such a project. Her background of training and experience as a nurse, in addition to two post-graduate years of training in child development and social work, equipped her with special knowledge of children and a sympathetic attitude toward them. Her earlier work showed her also to be endowed with two further requisites for leadership of the project: tremendous physical stamina and dedication to the welfare of children.

Because the Institute of Child Study was involved, its philosophy formed the basis of the rehabilitation programme. It is based on the concept of psychological "security," a theory developed by the late Dr. W. E. Blatz, the director of the Institute of Child Study for thirty-four years (9). This theory has been slightly modified by Flint, Millichamp, and Davis after further research into the ways in which security develops through infancy and early school years (45).

The Institute of Child Study is a faculty within the University of Toronto. It is essentially a research centre in which a variety of studies are made of children's growth and development. It has its own school with grades extending from nursery through Grade VI. A research staff and a parent education staff keep records on the children and are in close contact with their parents. In addition, for many years research has been conducted on a number of children outside the Institute, and the whole staff, including the teachers in the school, participate in research projects.

From 1953 to 1958, a complete research programme had been directed by the Institute towards a search for the basis of mental health in young children. Instead of seeking pathological symptoms, these studies had investigated the developmental health of children, and had formulated practical conclusions and principles of guidance in terms of the ways in which it could be promoted (45). Therefore, when we embarked on the project of helping seriously deprived children, we were able to apply our knowledge of the needs of well children. No child was to be diagnosed or typed in terms of mental illness, but rather was to be regarded as a unique individual with strengths and weaknesses which could be assessed. Once these qualities were determined, a practical programme of guidance would be put into operation which would emphasize the assets rather than the liabilities of the children. Gradually, as a child's strengths became more firmly established, his weaknesses should become less debilitating to his personality. Although the workers would need to be fully aware of the symptoms of illness displayed by each child, positive emphasis would constantly be put on developing his strengths.

To put such aims into practice, a conceptual framework was needed to serve as a guide, and our concept of "security" or "trust" was made to serve as a guiding principle. It is based on the belief that trust in others, and trust in oneself and one's world, form the core of mental health. The attitude of trust begins to develop in early infancy as a result of the care first given to the infant by his mother or mother substitute. With kindly care, order and meaning are given to a child's first experiences, and through his relationship to the person caring for him, he first develops trust in other people. Out of such relationships he forms an opinion of himself, and sees himself as a person of considerable worth. This feeling of self-worth, in turn, permits him to extend his confidence to more people and new experiences. The two requirements for mental health in early childhood are a relationship with a dependable, consistent adult (usually a mother figure) who can be relied on for care and encouragement, and the development of self-confidence which grows through the opportunity for independent action.

There is a definite sequence in the development of mental health. First of all, on the basis of care and guidance given him by his parents, an infant must develop a sense of dependence and trust. From his sense of trust in this world he gains a feeling of self-worth. This feeling in turn gives him the confidence to put forth effort and act independently in some circumstances. This independence of action, because it brings satisfaction from self-initiated effort, develops in the child a feeling of self-trust. "Dependent trust" (trust in others) and self-trust (a feeling of well-being about oneself and one's actions) are combined in a mentally healthy child.

Using the theory outlined above, we started a new programme in an old institution. Could a theory which emphasized health be applied successfully to a group of abnormal children? If it was to be successful, several major changes had to take place. First, the present staff members of the institution had to be either retrained or replaced in order to provide us with adults capable of giving a sense of dependent trust to these difficult youngsters. Our staff members had to be concerned with the children rather than with themselves, and had to be able to continue to give love and appreciation although rebuffed many times. They had to understand our philosophy and be able to take practical steps to apply it. They had to treat the children with such consistency and under such controls that the children could regard their world as dependable, as well as warmly comfortable. Further, although the children were beyond the early months of infancy, the staff would have to permit them to go through the early psychological development of very young infants and to grow slowly in emotional strength until they resembled normal children. This would be one of the most difficult things for even trained staff members to do, because the expectations of adults towards two- and three-year-old children are based on observations of normal children capable of acting their age.

Implicit in our approach was the conception of each child as a unique individual with potential for development at a pace suited to himself, with a need to have his capabilities recognized, at whatever level they might be. Inevitably, in dealing with large groups of children, the present staff had fallen into the habit of thinking of them as a group rather than as a collection of unique individuals. The children had never had any toys of their own, clothes had been shared by all, they had been herded into sections and kept there as groups. They had received no undivided affection, and nothing in their world had given them the feeling that they were unique.

In addition to changed attitudes amongst adults in charge of the children, a much larger staff was needed. Our earliest study (1957) had indicated that these children had broadly three ways of relating to their world. Some of them seemed most interested in people. Others seemed to get along best with material things, while a third group seemed content to watch, attempting no contact either with things or with people. The most direct approach to therapy appeared to be one that would take advantage of these different characteristics: those children who felt most comfortable with objects could be encouraged through playthings; others who liked people would be given the opportunity to talk and play with a staff member; while others would be permitted a longer time to watch, to assess, and finally to find a way to put some trust in their world. To use these techniques successfully a much larger staff was needed. In fact, a staff at least twice the size of the present one was essential. One adult for every three children was needed for effective guidance.

It was important that the staff recognize not only that the children were capable of doing things for themselves, but also that training in self-help had psychological value. Previously, no encouragement had ever been given to a child to put effort into play or to attempt to do such things as dress himself, feed himself, or use the toilet. Such effort, rewarded by the acquisition of competence in small tasks, greatly enhances a child's feeling of self-worth.

In order to broaden the limited environment in which the children were living, the building itself needed drastic remodelling. Partitions between each bed had to be removed, to permit children to communicate with each other. Toilets and wash basins were needed to start toilet training and to encourage the children to help themselves. Cupboards for clothing, and individual receptacles for each child's belongings had to be provided. Playrooms and toy shelves were needed to create separate play space in addition to sleeping rooms and eating quarters. Equipment was needed for play in the gardens.

The major problem of staff was tackled first. The total number of persons on the staff was doubled to 76, including maintenance and kitchen staff. This provided approximately one staff member for every child. Only a few of these new persons had had any training in child care; some had had no experience with children but showed enthusiasm to learn and open minds in their approach to children.° We employed a variety of means for training the staff, concentrating on giving the workers an understanding of normal development so they would recognize the deviations from normality or see immaturities in their proper perspective. Through an understanding of development, a worker would be better prepared to meet a child's needs by providing direction and using the techniques learned from supervisors. Central to all care was the idea that each child was unique in a way that had not previously been recognized or encouraged.

°Discussed fully in Chapter 5.

The feeling of uniqueness was now encouraged first by employing sufficient staff members who could give time for individual care and who could provide the opportunity for a child to feel somewhat dependent on one or two people whom he recognized as a relatively permanent part of his world.* In addition to staff members, a large group of volunteer "mothers" were trained, one of whom was assigned to each child. Their weekly visits and outings provided a further reinforcement of each child's sense of uniqueness and gave him a feeling that he was special to someone. Attention and affection from the staff and volunteers were to supply the previous lack of human contact, while firm controls were to be provided to give direction to the children's activity.

Secondly, the feeling of self-worth and uniqueness was to be enhanced by encouraging the child's effort to help himself. Bathrooms were installed with small toilets and washbasins, individual receptacles for clothing, and hooks for combs, tooth brush, wash cloth and towels, all designed so the children might reach and use them without help. Every effort was made to encourage the children to do things for themselves. Play materials were introduced, and concentrated effort was put forth both to teach the children how to use them and to help them achieve sufficient self-control to play purposefully with them. Instead of feeding and dressing all the children as quickly as possible, regardless of age, encouragement was given to those capable of making use of their own cupboards or drawers to dress themselves and feed themselves as adequately as they could.

Encouraging self-sufficiency was a slow process requiring patience to await children's interest and maturing skill, but it was an important part of the learning programme designed to build some feeling of self-worth and responsibility. The smallest infants, of course, were merely the recipients of care and love; they required social stimulation and encouragement to move ahead normally in their motor development.

To encourage a sense of uniqueness further, each child was given a toy of his own, to be followed by more when interest was shown. Clothes were made for each child, and were designed to look different from each other. In chatting with the children, the staff put considerable emphasis on these possessions. In order to enhance the opportunity for human interaction, playrooms with toys adequate for a variety of ages were provided, and small tables and chairs were set up, permitting the children to sit near each other in the dining room and enjoy a more normal living experience than formerly. Outdoors,

*Discussed fully in Chapter 8.

speech and co-operative effort were encouraged by the provision of wagons, tricycles, kiddy cars, sand play, water play, swings, and teeter totters.

The children varied in age from approximately three months to three years, so the programme had to be adapted to a variety of developmental levels. Because of the previous lack of stimulation, all the children showed some degree of retardation in development, the infant group demonstrating the least. For the youngest, roughly from three months to a year of age, much emphasis was placed on consistent physical care which provided tactile stimulation through holding, patting, hugging, kissing, rocking, etc. Social play through chatter, imitative games, tickling, singing, and smiling was encouraged. Toys to encourage activity both indoors and outdoors were made available, and encouragement was constantly given the children to develop such motor skills as sitting, creeping, climbing, walking, pulling, and pushing. The group of toddlers who were twelve months and older showed considerably more retardation than the youngest group and generally chronological age had to be disregarded in favour of developmental level. Those who showed any readiness were given every opportunity to help themselves in using the toilet, dressing, eating, and playing. Playrooms and playgrounds were readily adapted to meet each developmental level. The oldest and longest-deprived youngsters, ranging in age from roughly two and a half to three and a half years, were given more individual therapy to develop a feeling of dependency and stimulate some constructive interest in play activity and a sense of responsibility to care for themselves. In addition, an effort was made to get them beyond the confines of the institution and widen their living experiences within the community.

Assessing Changes

As the programme got underway, the children's reaction to it was used as a diagnostic yardstick whereby the staff could evaluate each child's potential for recovery under the system we had chosen. At the Institute of Child Study, two security scales had been developed, one for infants from birth to two years of age, and a second for children from two to five years. These mental health scales are essentially a diagnostic check list on which a variety of symptoms of behaviour, significant of mental health, are listed in terms of the theory of "security." To assess the degree of recovery of these deprived children, the rating forms were completed by the staff under the supervision of Miss Kilgour. The staff caring for the children then met in groups to discuss the significance of the results. Because the scales register both strengths and weaknesses, it was easy to see where the assets and liabilities of a child's personality lay. Once these were noted, a programme could be worked out for each child under which all the staff members in contact with him would encourage the child in his strong points, building upon them until they predominated and gradually compensated for the deep liabilities. More and more, as a child's strengths became obvious, every effort was made to encourage their development; the encouragement in turn led to feelings of well-being and self-worth. Because we knew that these positive feelings predominate in the personality of a well child, we considered that they should be developed in the deprived youngsters in order to improve their mental health.

Meeting the Changes

At first we expected that many months would elapse before any recognizable changes could be seen in the children. However, the children rapidly absorbed new experiences and grew mentally and emotionally in response to stimulation. Weekly, their demands for affection and attention became more intense. Weekly, they demonstrated a need for greater mental challenge. At the very beginning of the programme the children's greatest need was for love and attention, and the demand seemed insatiable. It was at this point that we introduced the volunteer "mothers" who could offer special attention to individual children and who could cater to their special needs. Gradually, as the children understood that there was someone who cared for them as unique individuals, they began to demonstrate their rudimentary feeling of well-being by pushing against the few limits and rules which had been set up. So insistent did their demands become that a situation close to bedlam developed. The children pushed, interrupted each other and adults, and ran aimlessly about throwing objects and yelling. Such behaviour required the staff to lay down strong controlling regulations, while continuing kindly and understanding care. Specific rules of behaviour which the children could understand were outlined for the nursery school playroom, and for the routines of eating, sleeping, dressing, and using the toilet. It appeared that these children, totally lacking in self-control and suddenly made aware of others as a potential source of interest, had become so over-stimulated by their contacts with each other that they were overly excited and erratic.

The adults were able to hold firm in their control while still encouraging self-expression through play materials, and commending responsibility in routines. Gradually the outer controls imposed by the adults were more and more accepted. Frequently now one would hear an adult saying "He can now be reasoned with." Very slowly, some of the children developed inner controls in varying degrees, and with them came a capacity to communicate with others in an effective way. The inner controls seemed to give the children a feeling of capability in taking on new experiences, and they demanded ever broadening horizons. The taste of home life which came through the contact with volunteers made them agonizingly aware of their own lack of parents. From time to time the question would arise, "Why do I not have a mummy and a daddy?" Out of the confusion of group living, a new personality would emerge almost daily, and another child would demonstrate so many signs of health that the possibility arose of placement in foster or adoptive homes.

Placement

Constant reassessment of the children on the Infant and Pre-school Security Scales,* made either in response to special needs or routinely every three months, revealed marked improvement in many of the children after the first year of treatment. Gradually, the more serious symptoms of disturbance dropped away and were replaced by positive signs of mental health. By the time eighteen months had elapsed, many of these formerly undeveloped youngsters showed sufficient signs of mental health to be considered ready for placement in homes. They had developed to the point where a treatment centre could offer them nothing more. The problem then was to find foster and adoptive parents who could love and accept such children as these, whose unusual past and dearth of living experiences would inevitably make them different from children reared in their own homes. The volunteer mothers, who had given the experience of a unique and highly beneficial relationship to the children they had chosen to care for, now provided another service. Many of them had become so attached to their charges that they wished to take them to their homes for permanent care or for adoption. The understanding and patience that they had shown the children had developed into love.

However, the fact had to be faced that despite apparent recovery,

*The full name of the Pre-school Scale is the Pre-school Mental Health Assessment Scale. Developed by Professor D. A. Millichamp of the Institute of Child Study, it is being refined prior to publication. The version given in the appendix (p. 155) is a working draft which has since undergone revision.

these children would undoubtedly be more vulnerable to stress than children reared at home. It was recognized that they would have a more difficult time growing up than most children. However, it seemed that at this point in their lives they could feel sufficient love and warmth toward a foster or adoptive family to reward the family's concern for them, and in the future they could settle adequately into a community and contribute to its welfare. Nevertheless, special parents had to be found who could recognize that children reared in an institution were different, and could offer special help when things were most difficult for them. Accordingly, a social worker was added to the staff who could help to choose particular homes to meet their specific needs.

5

The Staff

"A GOOD STAFF can work miracles—a poor staff can do nothing." These words from the supervisor in a moment of deep discouragement summed up our best hopes and bitterest frustrations. To develop a staff with sufficient understanding of the intellectual and emotional abyss in which the children had been living, to train them in techniques that would stimulate the children's minds and nourish their emotions, and to reinforce their staying power when the children became overly excited and endlessly demanding, these requirements took ingenuity, patience, and courage. The junior staff members needed constant direction and support from their seniors, the senior members needed constant reassurance and teaching from the supervisor, and the supervisor in turn needed encouragement and information from a variety of specialists who acted as consultants for different aspects of the treatment programme.

Specialized staff members were not as hard to obtain as the general staff required for the day-to-day running of the institution. The Toronto Hospital for Sick Children had offered aid in the treatment of physical disabilities; the research and guidance staff of the Institute of Child Study was always available with support and advice regarding the psychological care of the children; the nursery school staff of the Institute helped in setting up a treatment nursery school; a psychiatrist from a community treatment centre for children offered advice on children with particular problems; and the psychology department of the Catholic Children's Aid Society was available for developmental diagnosis. Part of the burden of administrative duties was carried by the Catholic Children's Aid Society, releasing the supervisor so that she could give more time to the things for which she was best suited and most needed: the care of the children and the teaching of the general staff and volunteers. An excellent dietician with experience in the Hospital for Sick Children took care of the household staff and building administration, and supervised the planning of the children's meals.

When Miss Kilgour had been appointed supervisor, she had inherited a staff which, with the exception of two recently appointed child development specialists, was too busy operating the institution to be aware of the importance of the emotional needs of the children. The staff had been concerned with the comfort of adults, geared to a routine enforcing physical cleanliness, and pleased by any quietness on the part of the children, since quietness was often construed as "goodness." Any child who demonstrated healthy qualities of rebellion or who showed sufficient initiative to make insistent demands on the staff was discouraged by being punished because such demands interfered with the staff's capacity to deal with the enormous task of keeping the children clean and fed. Thus needs of the staff had frequently taken precedence over the needs of the children, and the whole organization depended on arrangements made for the staff's convenience, covering the cooking and serving of meals, hours off and on duty, living accommodation, and the children's rest periods. The head of the staff, overwhelmed by the difficulty of finding sufficient personnel to give twenty-four hour care to the children, made every possible attempt to keep what staff members there were comfortable and happy.

While the ratio of approximately 38 adults to 85 children imposed a major problem, the difficulty was compounded since many of the staff had recently arrived from Europe and, not speaking English, were unable to communicate with each other or with the children. It may have been this inability to communicate, in addition to the need to hurry, which accounted for the almost complete lack of conversation between the adults and the children. The fact that these staff members usually stayed only a short while before moving on to another location undoubtedly affected the children adversely, leaving them confused and unrelated to any particular person.

These difficulties, added to the lack of awareness in the staff of the psychological needs of young children, made it impossible to treat the youngsters as individuals. Being constantly herded about in large groups left the children with virtually no regard for each other. As a result, they would trample on top of each other as if each were an inanimate object in the path of another's activity. Such children, almost impossible to organize and control, responded like frightened animals to harsh voices and rough physical handling. The staff seemed constantly on the verge of an exasperation which reflected their inadequacy.

Such were the situations and attitudes which had to be dealt with in order to change the programme to one which was child-centred and therapeutic. Working as we did from our knowledge of well children, and attempting to apply our theory of security (18) to these very young children, we recognized that their well-being depended on the capacity of the staff to help each of them. Therefore, thoughtful, dedicated, patient, and well-informed staff members were essential to the successful operation of this treatment centre. The problem was to find staff members who not only were capable of encouraging the children to become dependent, but who also could break through apathy and indifference, and accept hostility and erratic behaviour.

Furthermore, because the children ranged in age from three months to over three years, there was great variation in the degree of deprivation. Those children who had been in the institution for three years were obviously going to resist treatment much longer than the babies who had been there only a few months and who were ripe for a maternal person to give them affection and individual attention. Treatment was further complicated by the fact that some children had come from broken homes and some had undiagnosed physical defects. Their limited environment made it impossible to assess what degree of intelligence each might have.

Once the changes were started and an attempt made to explain the reasons for them, a storm of protest arose from the original staff. They could not understand or accept the new point of view since it was completely alien to their own ideas. Bitterness at the realization that their own efforts were inadequate, and resentment that they were expected to conform to a new regime made them hostile to the plan at the beginning. Highly authoritarian staff members were most critical of the new programme and tended to react to it by becoming more severe and rigid. This complete divergence of opinion regarding the care of the children made it impossible to attempt the long process of retraining necessary to establish a satisfactory attitude towards therapy. The only recourse was to dismiss many staff members at both junior and senior levels. Fortunately a small number of the original staff members remained who could tolerate the new ideas, accept the children's behaviour, and try to better understand its motivation.

When not only old staff members needed to be replaced but new staff had to be added as well, the state of emergency which arose almost produced panic. The budget had been increased to permit a staff double the original size. Very few experienced or trained people were immediately available, so it was necessary to take on a variety of persons who were available and who seemed to have an open mind to this approach to the children. As staff training started, and living with the children became a fact, many of these latter people also had to leave because they found it impossible to adapt to such a group of youngsters. This early upheaval in the staff aggravated the children's insecurity and made them even more difficult to deal with. Fortunately, as the months passed a core of staff members was developed, trained to administer specialized care; they became enthusiastic, eager, and dedicated people interested in planning the best possible kind of help for each child's needs. The institution became truly child-centred, and the complaints and grievances of the staff no longer threatened its future.

Viewed in retrospect, the change seems to have been relatively simple. But at the time the details of the daily planning, training, and coping with staff problems appeared nearly insurmountable, and most of the burden fell on the shoulders of the supervisor. Had it not been for her rare quality of leadership, the rehabilitation of the children might never have taken place. Her determination to place the welfare of the children above all else, her ability to plan minutely for changes while keeping the long-term goal in mind, her stamina and capacity to work twelve to fifteen hours daily in the first confused months: these were large factors in the success of the programme. If a carefully worked-out plan proved inadequate, she never hesitated to discard it immediately in favour of another. One of her greatest assets was her knowledge of child development, enabling her always to suit the therapy programme to the developing needs of the children, and providing a clarity of purpose which kept the goals of therapy clearly defined.

The first few months of treatment were very difficult for all staff members as they attempted to adapt to a new programme and a new philosophy. Regular meetings called by the supervisor to discuss the programme frequently became grumbling sessions at which the staff voiced their most irritating problems and then returned to the children, satisfied that they had at least been heard. Very gradually, as they realized that their dissatisfactions had a sympathetic hearing, they began to work together and were able to concern themselves with learning more adequate ways to help the children.

Over the first few months a stable staff hierarchy evolved. The supervisor, Miss Kilgour, was the general administrative head, taking responsibility for the overall operation of the institution and directing the programme of rehabilitation. It was she who worked out time-tables to permit the smooth functioning of each section, and she who decided on the best person for each job. She offered advice in constructing the more detailed time-tables required for each nursery unit. When programme changes seemed necessary or when a child needed special attention in order to continue his progress, she called in the proper specialists. In addition, she kept up a liaison with the community. She attended to the personal concerns of the staff members and made sure that all changes were interpreted to the staff to promote understanding and ensure as smooth an operating organization as possible. She saw that the day and night staff was so arranged that the day staff was much larger and more fully trained, since it was responsible for therapy and teaching. Planning the staff and volunteer training sessions, as well as doing some actual teaching and demonstrating, also constituted part of her duties.

Two other persons shared senior supervisory duties: a dietician and a nurse. The dietician supervised the maintenance of the building, took care of such emergencies as burst plumbing, kept a watchful eye on the condition of the building equipment and large toys, and supervised the activities of the household staff. Her experience in a children's hospital suited her admirably for the planning of the children's meals. In consultation with the supervisor, she worked out plans for the children's dining room.

The third senior staff member carried out general supervisory and liaison duties in the large, rambling two-storey building. She worked directly with the staff on duty, helping to keep communication free among the various nursery sections as well as between the upstairs and downstairs staff. She was alert to difficulties and failures in the programme, and kept the supervisor informed about the overall day-to-day successes and problems. In addition, because of her knowledge of the children (she was one of the former staff members) and her sensitivity to them, she was trained to work with individual children who needed special attention of the sort that could be given through individual play shared by an adult and a child. Such play makes use of toys while encouraging and appreciating a child's expression of emotion. Although it cannot be construed as play therapy in the recognized sense of the term, it certainly is therapeutic in outlook and effect.

The majority of the staff worked directly with the children, supervising their care, looking after their clothing, getting them in and out of the building for play and walks, talking to them, and showing interest in them. Gradually, as the number of children was reduced by placement in homes, and more attention could be given to an overall plan of care than had been possible in the first few months, a new group of women emerged whose duties were semi-supervisory. These women, the "unit mothers," began to take a more specialized and important role in the rehabilitation programme. Each was placed in charge of a group of staff and children, for which she was responsible. Each attended to time-tables in her own section, made sure that the children were getting adequate supervision, and looked after the provision of clothing and made sure it was kept in good repair. They attended staff meetings with the supervisors, and acted as liaisons between the supervisory and nursery staff. They were chosen on the basis of the demonstrated special interest in the programme and special sensitivity to the children. As no extra money was available to pay them more than the salary of the nursery nurses, added incentive was offered by the provision of a special uniform, which designated a certain degree of prestige.

When a nursery school was established in the garden coach house beside the main building, an additional four persons trained in child development and nursery techniques were added. This group functioned as a unit separate from the staff of the main building, but attended joint staff meetings to make sure that aims and techniques were the same in both sections. Later, the nursery school was used as a training centre for the whole staff.

Despite the development of a more or less fixed hierarchy in the staff, there continued to be many staff changes which were upsetting to the children, even six months after the beginning. We had to recognize that the slow progression of the children towards normal behaviour seemed unrewarding to hard-working adults who liked to see clearer gains from their efforts. The necessary intense concentration on meeting the needs of the children frequently made the adults feel that their own needs were being completely disregarded. We had to be careful to interpret our actions to the staff, and we constantly tried to make the staff feel that they had profitably invested part of themselves in the lives of the children. We attempted to show them that the children were doomed to a dreary future without their efforts at rehabilitation. Each person was vital to the success of the experiment.

Constant changes in programme were needed to meet the developing needs of the children, and these changes were always discussed and interpreted at staff meetings in order to avoid resentment. Time-tables were arranged in such a way as to guarantee as much consistency as possible in the relation between the staff and children, and yet consider the needs of the staff also. Finally, a pattern evolved whereby trained staff members worked five or five and a half days a week, to be replaced on the weekends by a permanent weekend staff. A permanent house mother was employed for a while to live in the building, take charge of the children on some of the weekends, and create a homier atmosphere, but after a few weeks the plan was abandoned because we could not find an adequate person for such a job. The caretaker was the only male figure constantly around the building, and his services were frequently extended to looking after certain difficult children who might benefit from a friendship developed with him. It was not unusual to see him, as he repaired toys, cut lawns, or set up equipment, accompanied by a sad waif or an eager boy, depending on the degree of recovery of the child.

One of the rewards of the hard work which the staff put into their jobs came from some of the humorous situations which arose and the laughter which was shared. One such incident occurred when we began to take the children out of the building and introduce them to a variety of experiences beyond the institution. Because the children were starved for such stimulation by the outside world, the staff often struggled to take out large numbers single-handed. Thus Flora, a unit mother, found herself accompanied by many small children one sunny afternoon. At our request, we had received a great variety of carriages in assorted states of repair which we needed in order to take infants or youngsters just learning to walk out for air. One large English pram, in a rather wobbly state, could accommodate three children sitting. This inevitably produced a problem of steering, but with patience it could be managed. Flora, with her solid Scottish amiability, put her full quota of three in the carriage and took along a fourth child who could toddle along beside her. As she pushed her load up the street, valiantly compensating for the list to the left, she created quite a picture. The children were varied in appearance from Oriental to blond Nordic. None looked much like Flora. As Flora approached a bus stop, where two well-dressed and rather prim women were waiting for transportation, they glared at her with disapproval. One turned to her companion and sniffed, "It's easy to see it's the baby-bonus she's after!"

Staff Training

Staff training involved a knowledge of child development, a recognition of deviation from normality, and an understanding of why these deviations might occur. It also included the acquisition of specific techniques for dealing with the children. Such a comprehensive objective was achieved in a variety of ways. One of the formal means by which we attempted to build a therapeutically oriented staff was a series of twenty evening lectures, attended by nearly all staff members, on specific techniques for dealing with young children at various stages of development. The staff discussions which followed on the lectures day after day seemed to add greatly to the skills of the group. Three of the senior members who were the focal points of these discussions were highly trained in child development and in practical techniques of dealing with young children. They were able to offer their knowledge to the others who had much less understanding. In addition, the resident nursery school was used as a training centre for all other staff members, so that a certain amount of consistency in attitudes and techniques prevailed throughout the institution. Visits to other day nurseries and child care centres gave an opportunity to observe not only how children behaved in these settings, but also how a programme could be adapted to meet the needs of young children. The research aspect of the programme also proved an excellent method of teaching staff members to be accurate observers and to understand the implications of the behaviour they were recording for each child. The Infant and Pre-school Security Scales listed a variety of types of behaviour which could be checked off as they applied to each child. Staff discussions following these ratings brought out the significance of the behaviour that overlay the feelings of a child. Such discussions, guided by the indications on the scales, further indicated the way to deal most adequately with the unique predispositions of each child.

In discussing the treatment programme we always attempted to relate our methods to theory and then outline practical measures to implement our theoretical conclusions. Therefore, the first step was to build a relationship under which the children could trust and depend on the staff. To do this, specific instructions were given that the children should have all the affection adults could muster and that as much attention as possible be devoted to each child in an attempt to make him feel unique. More time should be spent with each child, and the opportunity for talking, caressing, and encouraging effort should be taken during times when such routines as bathing, washing, dressing, and putting to bed were taking place. We suggested that the children should be held when possible, put on a knee when being dressed, tucked into bed with a pleasant little ritual, and talked to a great deal. Even with such specific instructions, misunderstandings crept in, owing to the inability of some staff members to understand the purpose of all this. Many incidents took place which were both discouraging and humorous.

One story which became a classic arose from a misunderstanding of the directions regarding the bathing of the youngsters. Bathing had always been a perfunctory routine for the children, carried out quickly with no regard for the fact that it might be enjoyable. In order to change the bath to a relaxed occasion which the child could enjoy and which the staff could use as a way of making pleasant contact with one child at a time, we suggested that all the children need not be bathed every day as formerly, but rather every other day or so. During the bath, the nurse should take the opportunity to show her interest in the child and share a pleasant time with him.

Thinking that her instructions had been straightforward and comprehended by all, Miss Kilgour walked about the building one evening to see if any appreciable rewards were obvious in the children's behaviour as a result of the changed attitude toward bath time. To her surprise she discovered one nursery where all the children had already been put to bed. No evidence of bathing could be seen, and the nurse was efficiently getting ready to leave as soon as the night staff appeared. When questioned about the bathing, the staff member naively stated that she had followed instructions that nightly bathing was not essential. So she had hurried to bathe her whole group the previous night and was now reaping the rewards of her efficiency, having put all the children to bed early to allow herself time to relax.

The Children's Response

We recognized that despite the increased staff looking after the children there were still too many children to be cared for by each person. Ideally we wanted each child to have some time in every day when he was alone with an adult, even if only for a few moments. Without some such opportunity we could not succeed in developing the feeling of uniqueness in each child. However, much to our surprise, even the little snatches of time that could be devoted to each child produced rapid and almost overwhelming results. Given a taste of affection and individual attention, the children demonstrated an insatiable hunger for more. Individually, they demanded more attention from adults. In groups, they gradually became more responsive to each other, to the point where their behaviour became excited and uncontrolled. Speech improved immeasurably but retained a peculiarly staccato quality. The noise level and pace of activity rose all over the building. There was a change in the nature of the sounds made by the children. The staff were overjoyed the first time they heard a real cry of anger rather than a disheartened wail, because it demonstrated that one of the children felt sufficiently intensely about something to express anger, and had sufficient confidence in the adults not to repress it. Despite the staccato and rather erratic quality of the children's speech, some expression began to appear in their voices. The bestowal of affection was paying off in an abundance of response.

After six months of the treatment programme, it became apparent that not only the younger children could respond to adults who were interested in them, but also eighteen of the hitherto most severely deprived older children. Most of these were over four years of age, and had appeared hopelessly unaware of others, erratic and aimless in their behaviour, and grossly defective in their intellectual skills. Now they were eager and able to respond to kindliness. Their apparent desire to receive attention, a passing caress, or commending word, helped the staff see through their peculiarities to the confused heart of a child in need of affection, direction, control, and a place to rest where he "belonged."

Introducing Controls

The confusion which arose when most of the children began to show some initiative, some interest in adults and each other, and some slight feeling of self-worth, was the result not only of stimulation from adults but also of some changes in the structure of the building. Partitions had been taken down between the cribs, and play space in special rooms provided toys for children at a variety of developmental levels. Encouragement was given to the children to attempt to help themselves in the necessities of eating and dressing, and the toilet and bathing routines. In a matter of a few weeks the children seemed to explode out of their state of lethargy and look around for things to do. The staff was completely taken by surprise, for they had not anticipated so early a need for outer controls, and the children were totally lacking in inner controls. For a few weeks, life in the treatment centre

became a disconcerting whirl of frightened children milling about
with no direction or purpose to their activity. Immediate action was
needed on the part of the staff. Controls had to be imposed in order
to prevent total chaos, yet care had to be taken to prevent use of
harsh methods as a result of the staff's inability to understand the
nature of the problem. Methods of control had to be devised which
could remain consistent with our theory of developing security in the
children. Because of our history of nursery training at the Institute
of Child Study, we had a ready-made plan of discipline consistent
with our theory and effective with normal children. This was Dr.
Blatz's theory of allowing the child to make decisions and accept the
consequences of his behaviour (9).

Briefly, the implications of this plan are as follows. Each child is
regarded as a "learning" being, always in a situation whose meaning
he learns to comprehend. If he is learning acceptable things from his
environment, he reflects it in appropriate behaviour which is reinforced
by adult approval. Should he be learning unacceptable behaviour
from his environment, this too is reflected in inappropriate behaviour
and is discouraged by adult disapproval, or by lack of satisfactions
resulting from the activity. Furthermore, the adult who guides him
teaches desirable behaviour by altering an unfavourable environment
to one which better suits his needs and favours the selection of appropriate behaviour. Each moment of life invites action and offers choices
for a child to make in the course of his activity. Encouraged by an
environment which directs his choices to desirable behaviour, he reaps
the reward of enjoyment and self-satisfaction which arise from his
chosen course of action. Hence a future choice in the same direction
is reinforced. On the other hand, should he make the choice of disruptive and unacceptable behaviour, his satisfactions are minimized
and his enjoyment so curtailed that a future choice of such behaviour
is discouraged. Such a plan of discipline presupposes a child whose
mind is ready to learn, who can take responsibility for making minor
decisions in very limited areas, and who is capable of understanding
the implications of the consequences of his actions and of learning
from them. It permits the slow development of responsibility within
a child and opens the way for the maturing of inner controls.

The theory of discipline just outlined has no place in it for physical
punishment. The child is given a choice of behaviour which is accepted
by the adult who merely makes sure that the choice is carried out.
It is up to the adult in charge to make sure the choices open to a child
are within the scope of his maturity and, therefore, that it is possible

for him to accept the consequences of his choice. For example, should a child playing with a group of other children disrupt their play and upset the children, he is given a choice of either remaining in the group and conforming to its standards or going by himself. As the adult acts only as an interested arbiter and guide to help the child carry out his choice, the adult-child relationship is never jeopardized by force or threats of punishment. Rather, a friendly, trusting relationship between the two is always possible.

This plan of discipline can be progressively adapted to provide for greater maturity as the child changes mentally and physically. Broader and broader choices can be offered as he gains control of himself and better understands his environment. Such a plan, however, requires adults in control of it who are capable of arranging conditions for learning with long-term goals in mind. Short-term goals, emphasizing immediate conformity, threaten the long-range learning of responsibility and the building of inner controls. Because of their immaturity and their confused state of mind, the children in the McNeil Home were at first unable to respond to such a plan of discipline.

Therefore, the application of the plan in our institution required ingenuity and planning beyond that needed for normal children, in order to arrange conditions for learning whereby opportunity for making choices could be adapted to progressive levels of maturity. In this way a child could take progressive responsibility for his own actions as he developed. The immaturity of these institutionalized children and the unevenesses in their development at first precluded their taking any responsibility, even for feeding and dressing themselves. All-pervasive adult controls were necessary to give direction and meaning to the children's activity. Four-year-old children needed to be supervised like babies and gradually exposed to ever broadening experiences of normal life. Only as they learned to cope with very simple choices (e.g., what toy to play with) could they be given an opportunity to assume a little responsibility for their own behaviour. Only very gradually could inner controls develop and external ones be loosened. Our long-term goal of developing self-control and some degree of self-discipline seemed indeed a long way off.

Methods to control the children's first burst of expression of their "aliveness" consisted in large part of specific and detailed rules of behaviour which were carried out consistently in every aspect of their lives (eating, sleeping, washing, dressing, playing). In this way as their activity gained direction, their world became reassuringly predictable. The tempo of activity once more abated, but the quality of the behaviour was healthier than at the earlier stage and gave the opportunity for the staff to recognize more facets of each child's personality and pay more attention to individual needs.

Nine months after the treatment programme had been initiated, the children were responding so satisfactorily that they had gained greatly in emotional and physical maturity and in their ability to express themselves. Such development made continual changes in the overall programme necessary if their growing needs were to be met and if they were to continue making progress. These changes tested the patience of even the best staff members, and required constant interpretation. Other than the senior group, the one sustaining staff group which did not change comprised the four nursery school teachers. They had had training before becoming part of the institution, and they were challenged by the task of adapting a nursery school programme to the needs of such a group. The constancy of these teachers was a great benefit to the children, for it helped give consistency to their lives. Each of the children could look forward to a common experience with the same people each day. The teachers also proved a source of inspiration to the other staff, who benefitted from their suggestions regarding the organization of routines and the use of play equipment. The adaptation of nursery school principles to the institution quarters itself provided relief from some of the pressures on the staff and promoted a comfortable environment for the children.

After the programme had been running for a year, fifty children remained in care. A core of staff, enthusiastic about the children, carried the weight of treatment, and a fairly clearly defined pattern of care was evolved. We finally saw some hope for real success in rehabilitation. It was still necessary to outline time-tables with detailed and specific directions in order to avoid misunderstanding and confusion.* Unit mothers, each responsible for five or six children, had proven their worth. In order to assure their staying, they were permitted every weekend off, and a regular weekend staff took over. Some senior staff members always had to be on duty, for emergencies requiring their attention frequently arose. Both the unit mothers and the senior staff members attempted to become an important focus in the children's lives, the unit mother aiming towards providing sufficient warmth to take the place of a real mother. Often she would spontaneously take a child home for a weekend. Such weekends came to be highly valued by the children. Special clothes made by the unit mother herself might appear in the children's wardrobe.

*See appendix.

The number of children in the various units was reduced to the smallest possible, and as a result, adult-child relationship showed decided gains with less friction. By the end of the first year a gratifying amount of enjoyable interaction was going on between the children and staff. Junior staff members had become sufficiently interested to spontaneously arrange their own discussions about certain groups of children in their care.

Fifteen months of changes finally found only thirty-nine children left in our care. As the number of staff remained constant, this permitted us to give more careful attention to the individual needs of the remaining children.

A system of placement in different units was worked out according to what was termed a "family plan." Now, instead of placing children of roughly the same age in one group, we put them into a group where there was a variety of ages, more closely allied to the brother-sister constellation which might be found in a home. We thought that the younger ones could learn more mature behaviour through imitation of the older ones than they would learn in a group of contemporaries. Conversely, the older ones would have an opportunity to become protective towards the little ones. We hoped that they might develop a sense of responsibility to shape some of their behaviour into more acceptable channels given the incentive to be the oldest of a group. The role of the unit mother changed somewhat as she worked more closely with a smaller number. A unit mother encouraged the children in her group to become deeply attached to her. She did special things with each of them, such as taking them to the shoe store, to the barber, or to pick out clothes for special occasions. She set aside time every day for each child, to be spent alone with him reading, playing, or talking while she mended. She would come in and put her special children to bed, arrange rooms, and provide special furniture. She might rock a child, cut his nails, wash his hair, or take him for a walk.

It was at this point that we were able finally to adopt criteria for placing each child in a particular unit. Because of her own personality qualities, a unit mother might be infinitely helpful to one child, but incapable of helping another. It was difficult to convince the rest of the staff of this. Indeed, it often took considerable time before a unit mother was able to accept this fact herself and act upon it. However, once the benefit was apparent to all concerned, we were able to select a child with a personality acceptable to a particular unit mother. This was our first criterion for placement. Secondly, we were able to select for each unit children with varying degrees of emotional damage, in the hope that the most seriously upset might gain stability through living with children whose behaviour was more acceptable and more predictable. We tried to work out a "family" group of three or four children which seemed of the greatest advantage to each one, with which the unit mother felt comfortable, and which she was capable of managing.

Under this programme, the staff dug into their work with determination and sensitivity. Gradually the most hopeless-seeming child appeared to respond to well-planned treatment. As sufficient improvement began to show, child after child was moved on to foster or adoptive homes. Unit mothers were able to invest a great deal of their emotional lives in special children and enjoyed the reward of seeing themselves supplanted in the children's affection by an exciting mother and father. Many a quiet tear was shed by a staff member who had worked for months with some unsuspecting youngster who now went eagerly off to his new home with his new parents.

As the number of children was reduced with the passing months, the remaining staff continued with stamina and dedication to work with the most difficult children whose behaviour still seemed incomprehensible. Now there was no longer any question of someone leaving because things did not suit her particular needs. The needs of the children were uppermost in everyone's mind, and the whole organization, from supervisor to caretaker, seemed dedicated to the purpose of making the children well enough to leave the institution in which they had remained so long.

6

Health, Food, and Daily Care

OUR MAJOR CONCERN in transforming institutional care to a treatment programme was the health of the children. Both mental and physical health had been seriously impaired; it was impossible to say which had suffered most from the institutional environment. The outward symptoms of poor health were depressing. Chronic infections, mainly colds, affected the entire group. All the children were pallid and listless. Their eyes seemed abnormally large and dull, staring from immobile, expressionless faces. Their co-ordination between eye and hand was grossly inadequate for their age; those who could walk or run had an uneven, erratic gait, and their feet tended to be flabby. Weak muscle tone and limp hands interfered with their ability to grasp. Many of the children compulsively rolled and twisted their hands from the wrists. All had poor posture. Heads were generally thrust forward, shoulders drooped, and arms hung limply down at their sides. Their movements were of two extreme types: either slow or else tense and erratic. Their general appearance was that of malnourished children, and most of them appeared underweight. It was evident that any change promoting better physical health would inevitably be reflected in mental health.

We therefore set about to plan a programme which would provide not only a healthful physical environment but also a challenging and rewarding psychological milieu. The youngest children, unable to toddle, were provided with sufficient clothing and equipment (such as carriages and playpens) to allow them two daily periods outdoors, winter or summer, whether they were put out on a verandah in a carriage or playpen, or taken for a walk. More variety was added to their diet, and more time was allowed for feeding each child. They were placed in high-chairs when given solids, and held in arms for bottle feeding. When old enough, the children were encouraged to hold a spoon and to attempt to feed themselves. An opportunity was provided for play with grown-ups, with other children, and with toys. Walkers and "jolly-jumpers" encouraged motor skills preliminary to creeping and walking. The children were allowed to move out of their own wards and creep or push a walker through the halls and into other nearby rooms.

Similarly, for the group of children who were walking, a balanced programme of physical activity, rest, and responsibility was worked out. At least two daily periods of vigorous outdoor activity were planned, to be followed by more subdued indoor play. Quiet and boisterous periods of indoor activity were alternated. The total day's activity was divided into *routines* and *play*. The routines took care of the necessities of social living and included dressing, going to the toilet, bathing, eating, and sleeping. For each routine, clear-cut procedures were laid down which the children were expected to follow. Conformity was the goal. On the other hand, play activity offered the child freedom through which he might express his strongest feelings and exercise his uniqueness in a tolerant atmosphere. Once a procedure including play and routine was worked out for a whole day, the plan was consistently adhered to. This regularity gave both the staff and the children the security of knowing what step to anticipate next, and it provided a comfortable "anchor" to their activity. Further, it helped to orient the children realistically in time, giving meaning to such occasions as "getting-up time," "breakfast time," "play time," "toilet time," "lunch time," "sleep time," and so on. This kind of orientation was relatively new to them.

Routines were regarded as learning situations through which the children could acquire the simple skills needed to take care of some of their smallest needs, and through these achievements feel the satisfaction of being responsible for part of their lives. Dressing oneself, cleaning one's teeth, getting ready for bed, going to the toilet, and feeding oneself in an acceptable manner provide exciting challenges for a pre-school child, as long as the tasks are not made overwhelmingly difficult. We carefully controlled their complexity and made sure that the expectations were not above the child's capacity. Awkward fingers were not expected to do up buttons or pull on snow boots; socially immature children were not asked to sit together for meals or to control their desire to talk and tease one another.

The routines were arranged so that an adult would be nearby to give a hand with a problem before the child became too frustrated to deal with it successfully. The volatile child who was easily stimulated by social contacts was protected by being kept in relatively small groups when eating, sleeping, or dressing. The immature, bewildered child was helped by having the details of taking care of himself simplified and carried out to a greater extent by an adult. Every child was encouraged to put forth some effort and to pay attention to whatever was taking place. Beyond this, if he was considered capable of making an active effort, he was encouraged to do some things for himself—for example, wash his hands, brush his teeth, dry himself, pull on a rubber, comb his hair, feed himself, wipe his mouth—all the endless succession of trivia which engulfs a large portion of a young child's life. In order to foster the dependent relationships which are the foundation of mental health, we stressed co-operation between adults and children in carrying out the steps of the routines. Sometimes, long after a child had proved himself capable of doing a great deal for himself, the staff deliberately continued to do more for him than necessary believing that to foster a dependent relationship was more crucial to his mental health than the immediate development of skills.

For each of the five daily routines (eating, sleeping, going to the toilet, bathing, dressing), a procedure was established for the children to follow. For example, when a child was getting dressed he was expected to start with underclothes and proceed to socks, pants or dress, and sweater. If he were going outdoors, he should first put on his leggings, then snow-boots, top coat, scarf and hat. The regularity of following these same steps day by day enabled the child to grasp the succession of the activity and to carry out a large part of it without specific adult direction.

The pattern also enabled us to work out a plan of discipline whereby a child could be brought to understand the consequences of failing to carry out the procedure. Such consequences could be arranged without any emotion on the part of the adult, such as anger or disapproval, while the onus of making the choice of behaviour rested with the child. Hence he could, over a period of time, develop a degree of self-discipline. For example, if a child were dressing to go outdoors to play, and failed to do so properly because he was distracted by the other children around him, his behaviour was likely to deteriorate into overly-social boisterous teasing, which disrupted the dressing activity not only for himself, but for the other children. In such a case, he might be sent off for a few minutes by himself to return and dress later. If he procrastinated and was not willing to expend some effort, even with an adult helping him, he could be reminded of the next step, and that this was necessary before he could go outdoors to play. Continued failure would result in his missing outdoor play.

It was the youngest children with the least institutional experience who responded positively to their new experiences in the shortest time. The plan of discipline had meaning in their lives, and not many months had passed before they developed the beginnings of self-discipline. But the more severely damaged children remained immature and incapable of making choices for many months. They needed to rely on the adults to make the choices which would give direction to their behaviour. Self-discipline for them was a long way off.

Although each routine was a part of the total day and complemented the others in the overall plan of teaching the children how to cope effectively with their world, it also had a plan and a goal of its own. Consequently, we tended to talk about the routine aspects of the programme as if each were an entity. We evaluated the progress of each child within this framework, frequently commenting that, "Ellen is doing well in 'washing' now," "Janice is showing improvement in 'eating,'" or "Allan is still having great problems in 'sleep.'"

Our goals for the routine of dressing were two-fold: first, to encourage each child to help himself as far as he was able; and second, to teach each child to be attentive to a task until it was completed. Success in these tasks would result in a feeling of achievement that was a valuable asset to mental health. In order to carry out the plan, certain equipment had to be constructed, consisting of an individual cubicle for each baby's clothes, and a cupboard with accessible hangers for the clothes of each of the older children. As the children were moved into small "units" of their own, a separate chest of drawers was added. In this fashion, each child's clothing could be kept separate. As they grew older, they could readily take out or put away their own clothes.

Routines for bathing and using the toilet aimed at the same goals as dressing routines, i.e., competence in taking care of oneself and the enjoyment of doing so. A "do-it-yourself" environment was designed. Small toilets and wash-basins were provided which the children could use without adult help. Hooks on which each child placed his washcloth, towel, tooth brush and comb were easily accessible. Thus it was easy to encourage a child to help himself, and the children derived considerable satisfaction from these activities.

Toilet training had been an unhappy and unsatisfactory affair in the past, as staff had often hurried on their rounds without sufficient time to attend to the children properly. Many of the children had been left on "potties" far too long in an attempt to catch bowel movements. As a result, there existed among many of the children a negative attitude towards toilet training, which had to be overcome by the new staff before the children could be expected to be continent. Small toilets provided an intriguing challenge to many of them, and an unhurried attitude permitted the children to relax. Before long, the younger children, fifteen months and a little older, were responding to training. In the following months the oldest children, around three years of age, began to achieve success.

Sleeping and bed time, prior to this therapeutic programme, had hardly been differentiated from any other part of the children's day. Because they had spent so much time in their beds, sleep came as an escape from boredom rather than as the satisfaction of a need for relaxation and rest. In the new plan, rest time and bed time were made meaningful and enjoyable parts of the children's lives, coming at the same time every day, at the end of periods of activity. The schedule called for rising at 6:30 to 7:00 A.M., noon rest starting at 11:30 A.M., and a bed-time hour at night (6:00 P.M. to bed, 7:00 P.M. lights out). We discovered that when they started to respond to treatment, the children required more rest than children living with their families. Social interaction resulted in highly excited behaviour. A break in their activity provided by rest cut down on some of the excitement. We knew that the children needed rest or sleep when a high tempo of excitability swept through the building. We made every possible effort to provide a quiet evening period prior to sleep. The children were washed, taken to the toilet, dressed in their pyjamas, and put into their beds. Soft music was played through a public address system to help them relax. The six o'clock bed-time hour obviously was too early (particularly in the summer) to expect them to go immediately to sleep, but we wanted them to be relaxed and quiet. The idea of "toy-carts" was evolved for the older children. Tables laden with toys were wheeled from bed to bed in response to a child's request. Volunteers took care of the toy-carts for each room; this satisfied the children as they played quietly on their beds. At 7:00 P.M. lights were turned out, blinds drawn, children tucked in, and everything quieted down for evening sleep. Those children who were unable to settle quietly were moved to another room where their restlessness would not interfere with the group.

Although the food provided had been adequate, the routine of eating had been perfunctory, providing minimal satisfaction for the children. The shortage of staff before the changes took place had necessitated feeding each child as fast as possible. To economize on time, the food had been prepared the same way for all ages, except for the tiniest babies. Soft food stirred together in a dish was spooned into each child as he sat or stood in his bed. A child who desired to feed himself had his hands held out of the way to prevent him slowing down the process. The hungriest child, who cried when he saw food coming, was punished by being made to wait until the last. Meanwhile his screams resounded throughout the feeding period, creating an atmosphere of distress which added to the pace. The former staff, unaware of the significance of his behaviour, had hoped he would learn that patience was rewarded.

There had been little variety in food from day to day, supper invariably consisting of sweetened porridge. Furthermore, because of the emaciated appearance of the children, there had been a real insistence that each child eat his full quota, regardless of how he might be feeling from day to day. Despite the limited enjoyment, eating was the only satisfaction the children had. It temporarily relieved the drabness of their lives and gave them fleeting contact with an adult who did something for them.

Such a situation needed immediate attention. A new programme based on the needs of normal children was begun, under which the whole attitude of both the children and staff towards food and eating would be changed. Where before children had merely ingested food like animals, they could now regard eating as an aesthetically satisfying experience. Three clearly defined goals were kept in mind: the first, to set the children on the road to good health; the second, to prove that food can be interesting and enjoyable—that taste, colour, and texture all add to life's pleasures. A third goal was that the children gradually learn to accept a wide variety of foods as preparation for living in the broader community beyond the institution.

At first it was necessary to continue feeding the children in their own nurseries, but every effort was made to separate eating from the activities which preceded or followed it. The youngest children were taken from their beds or play activity and either held or put in high chairs. While given a bottle they were cuddled. Those children who were able to sit up were given a small table and chairs at which four or five might eat together with an adult. This arrangement was to provide social interaction among the children and to create a friendly atmosphere in which to eat under the supervision of a helpful, interested grown-up.

Because the children were having to make tremendous adaptations to many changes of staff and programme, few changes in diet were made in the first few weeks. The dietician, familiar with the difficulties of feeding younger children, looked for ways of making a new diet acceptable. A greater variety was desirable for all of them. For the older children, a gradual change in food textures was planned from pureed, to chopped, to diced pieces. Attention was given to variation in both colour and flavour, so that these differences could be as attractively presented as possible. Whenever a new food was to be introduced, it was always served with a well-liked familiar food. For example, at supper time the accustomed amount of sugar was gradually reduced in the porridge, and along with it would be a very small serving of some new food, such as creamy eggs, macaroni and cheese, or sandwiches. (Sandwiches met with wide acceptance, probably because of the children's familiarity with bread.) Rusks were presented to give some badly needed practice in chewing. Snacks of fresh fruits and cookies became part of the daily routine. Desserts were introduced slowly over a period of weeks.

The children benefitted at once from the larger staff, which permitted a more leisurely pace at meal time and allowed more consideration for individual differences in appetite. Each staff member directed and controlled the small group at her own table and, as the children developed, encouraged them to feed themselves and finally to serve themselves. The dietician had to help many of the staff members overcome their earlier habits of feeding the children. Many could not resist mixing all the food together to disguise the flavour, colour, or texture of some unfamiliar vegetable or meat. The value of the children tasting and recognizing each food had to be explained and the idea discouraged that food was necessary only to fill the children.

As soon as the number of children was reduced to sixty-seven by the return of some of the temporary wards to their own parents, it was possible to provide dining-room space entirely separate from nursery wards. The advantage of a separate dining room was worth a great deal of thought and planning. First, any opportunity of relieving the children's boredom with their surroundings by getting them out of their own rooms greatly added to their emotional well-being and enabled the staff to cope with them more adequately. Secondly, we wished to establish the attitude in the children's minds that meal-time was different and separate from the rest of the day. The children should learn to associate a special atmosphere, procedure, and enjoyment with eating.

The routine of eating provided an opportunity to motivate the children to help themselves and gradually to gain some self-control. The children were usually eager to eat and would therefore willingly participate in an established procedure. The fact that they ate together in a pleasant atmosphere provided incentive to accept the rules. New dishes and cutlery were bought and they added to the enjoyment of the procedure. The opportunity to use utensils, such as knives and forks, spurred the children to acquire the necessary skill. Small servings of food attractively presented avoided discouragement for any child who did not enjoy food, while the children who were enthusiastic eaters were encouraged to eat several servings. The acceptance of new foods was easy when servings were small. In case of an eating problem, desserts were used as motivation for completing meals. Completion of one first course permitted two desserts (small); completion of two first courses permitted three desserts. Because servings were kept very small, this was considered a reasonable requirement. Desserts were usually a favourite food.

A definite routine for meal time was established and followed consistently in every detail. The children were able to master it and take the responsibility themselves for carrying it out. "Get bibs, stand behind chairs, hands behind back, all say grace together, sit down, wait turn to be served." Each step was planned to become a satisfactory and enjoyable part of a child's world. The children very quickly learned the routine and rapidly developed their skills and interest. Two separate sittings, half an hour apart, permitted the youngest children to eat separate from the older ones, eliminating some of the excitement of social contacts, and permitting the children to pay greater attention to eating. The fewer the children sitting with one adult, the more relaxed and controlled was the dinner hour. Rules of behaviour needed to be set out. "Hands behind backs" while saying grace eliminated the problem of grabbing for food when the children first came to the table. A noisy or excited child would have to eat alone. The rule was, "if one disturbed the other children, then it was necessary to eat alone." Such a rule became an effective teaching device in the development of self-control. The desire to remain with the larger group while eating was very strong and proved to be sufficient motivation for the children to strive for control of their behaviour.

At first it was necessary for the staff to "patrol" the dining rooms, moving from one child to another, giving physical assistance and discipline. After a few weeks, the children were settled enough that each adult could sit down and supervise one group at a table. This arrangement reduced some of the activity and created a more friendly attitude at meal times. Control was being gradually transferred from adults to children. When new foods were introduced initially, they generally were met by gagging and spitting, or they were thrown to the floor. Gradually, the unfamiliar became accepted. Carrot sticks and celery first elicited resistance because of crisp texture. The children having had little practice in chewing seemed incapable of using their jaws and teeth. Rusks were offered to stimulate the desire to chew. After five months, celery and carrot sticks were eaten enthusiastically. At first we saw cautious acceptance, then eventually the spread of enthusiasm for new and different things. One child imitated another until the general tone of meal time was one of enthusiasm.

The younger children accepted new foods more rapidly than the older ones and their eating habits developed an acceptable pattern sooner. Because all the children were well beyond the level of physical maturity needed to feed themselves, such skills were mastered very rapidly. When the first thrill of mastery was over, they began to be restless and had to be permitted, one by one, to get up from their table and go to a central serving table for their desserts. Thus they relieved the tension created by the effort of sitting still.

This, in turn, led to the necessity of imposing some social controls. Once physical skills were mastered and new foods generally accepted, the children turned their attention to another thrilling aspect of their world—their companions. Previously, other children had been merely a frustration, an impediment frequently standing between them and some short-term goal. After a few months of treatment, they began to awaken to the fascination of other personalities. For the first time, they seemed to see their companions as interesting facets of their universe. Their reaction, when gathered in a group of any size (in the dining room, for instance) was one of high excitement. For this reason, the groups were kept as small as possible. Three or four children sometimes ate their meals in a hall, aside from the main group. Particularly volatile children sometimes ate away from the main group for several weeks, in order to relieve them of pressures with which they could not cope. As time went on, special units were set up for some of the oldest, most deeply disturbed youngsters, and they habitually ate only with two or three children of their own unit. Their relative isolation not only reduced the pressures on them, but also permitted the remainder of the group in the dining room a more relaxed, leisurely atmosphere.

After six or seven months, when food had become intriguing to the children, they began to ask questions about it. Appetites increased and the children looked very much better. A notable average weight gain of five pounds was recorded, whereas prior to the treatment programme no gain in weight had been recorded for the previous six months. Several kinds of compulsions appeared among the children. Generally they disliked wet or sticky hands and would not continue with a meal until they were wiped. New terry-cloth bibs became an essential part of their mealtime, and at first the children were greatly concerned that these be kept clean. "Dirty, dirty," was the expression of those children who could talk whenever a scrap of food found its way to a bib.

Another compulsion appeared which seemed to be a tag-end of former habits of care. Whenever a familiar food was served in a serving dish, the children seemed to have a frantic desire to see the bottom— no dish could return to the kitchen with anything left in it. They would indiscriminately stuff themselves and gobble down food until the serving was quite empty. Later, they seemed easier about food and were unconcerned if some was left to go back to the kitchen.

After five months on the new feeding routine, the excitement of eating together had been controlled, and the staff felt sufficiently confident to add a few frills. Birthday cakes with candles were introduced. At first, the children saw no association between the birthday cake and the individual for whom it was made. They were frightened of the lighted candles. When served the cake, they ate it with caution, some attempting to eat the candles too. It was only after the fourth birthday cake that some recognition began to dawn for some children. A three-year-old blew out his candles and with widened eyes exclaimed, "All mine." Gradually, curiosity replaced caution. Whenever a birthday cake was placed in front of a child, the others would rush to the table to admire and exclaim over it. Eventually, children from the other dining rooms were included in the celebration by being invited to come to see and sample the cake. Gradually, other special days were celebrated at mealtime—often by the use of decorations. For example, Hallowe'en pumpkins were used for decorations. These had been hollowed out and made into Jack-o-lanterns during nursery school time.

After seven months of the new programme, mealtime had become a pleasant, smoothly functioning routine, enjoyed by staff and children alike. Discipline for unacceptable behaviour had almost completely disappeared. Few children were being removed from the dining rooms. A new stage of maturity was evidenced by the children's discriminating in their tastes and expressing likes and dislikes of various foods.

We were encouraged by changes in the children's behaviour during mealtime. Such changes were reflections of the general improvement in well-being, and each child showed an increased capacity for individual response. An example of a child who showed a remarkable increase in self-control and enjoyment of eating was Joseph, who was two years old when we went into the institution. He was a poor eater, with exaggerated behaviour problems during mealtimes. He was in a state of chronic anxiety at the sight of food, screaming with impatience to get at it but not enjoying it when it came. He cried off and on throughout the meal and whenever a new food was offered to him he would fuss and fret, spitting out and crying between mouthfuls. He still needed a bottle.

Seven months later there was some slight improvement in his eating habits. He was able to give up his bottle and became much more co-operative about the dining procedure. He could accept familiar foods. New foods were accepted reluctantly over a period of time. If he was tired, he still fussed and fretted. He still objected to waiting for meals, showing his resentment by impatience and restlessness. He now wanted to feed himself and resented an offer of help.

After a further four months, although he was still a difficult and impatient little boy who demanded meals immediately, there was a marked improvement in his attitude towards food. He was now enthusiastic about most foods and would no longer protest about new ones. He was generally co-operative and could use a spoon efficiently when feeding himself. After eighteen months of treatment, his attitude towards eating and the dining room procedure was generally co-operative and pleasant. He was eating well and with enjoyment.

7

The Many Functions of Play

NOW THAT the total organization of the institution had been changed, play could be deliberately used as a therapeutic tool in the rehabilitation of the children. Play had a five-fold contribution to make to their development. Through adult acceptance and encouragement, and the enforcement of limits in play situations, children could be taught that there are dependable, supportive, and loving adults in their world. Through the challenge of a toy and the opportunity to make simple choices among playthings, they would be stimulated mentally. An awareness of the interesting possibilities inherent in the toys would result in greater ability to concentrate. Emotional satisfaction could be derived from their successful achievement of whatever goals they had set themselves with the play materials. And success would lead to a feeling of self-worth and security. Social relations should also show improvement in a controlled playroom setting which prevented overstimulation. "Controlling" the playroom setting meant limiting the groups using each playroom to very small numbers and giving each child a great deal of attention. Finally, a play programme would make a direct contribution to physical health. Outdoor activity particularly should bring about marked improvement.

Encouraging Dependent Relationships

When first introduced to play materials, most of the children were indifferent or apathetic. The few who showed interest and curiosity usually romped wildly from one toy to another, touching them and tossing them about. To overcome these deficiencies, individual play sessions were started with each child. In this way we achieved two goals. Since it was essential for an adult to be constantly with a child showing him how to choose and to use the toys without destroying them, this closeness could also be used to build a dependent relationship. While teaching the constructive use of play materials, an adult could accept the child's deviant behaviour without reprimanding him, at the same time redirecting him to more acceptable and rewarding behaviour. She would act as both guide and instructor but also give affection whenever it seemed appropriate. It was hoped that this relationship would initiate a feeling of dependent trust, which later should be sufficiently expandable to be transferred to a nursery school play supervisor in a larger and freer environment.

With this plan in mind, we set up throughout the building several small playrooms containing simple toys. Certain members of the staff, considered to be the most sensitive to the needs of the children, were selected to supervise groups during play sessions. They were not necessarily trained in psychology, social work techniques, or play supervision, but their effectiveness proved itself rapidly as they began to work with the children. Admittedly, those people trained in nursery school techniques, whose work had a basis of psychological understanding, proved on the whole to be most effective with this kind of work.

At first, simple objects and pictures were presented to the children, because their knowledge of the world was almost non-existent. Fruit, vegetables, animals, cars, household equipment and furniture, etc. were named, and in this vicarious fashion the children learned what to call them. Gradually, more complex play materials were added which had short-term goals readily understood by the children. Such toys as colour cones, blocks, simple puzzles, and cars gave the satisfaction of quick completion of whatever goal a child set himself. Once the children had learned to concentrate on this kind of toy, a little more complex material was added, such as scissors and magazines from which to cut pictures, which were then pasted on paper. Immature muscular control made these activities much more difficult for them than for normal children.

The initial part of the programme proved a good preparation for the next stage: the coach-house nursery school. Here the children were introduced to a playroom with adults and one or two other children. The old coach house was on the institution grounds at one end of the west garden, and had been part of the original Victorian establishment. It was a large two-storey building with plenty of big windows, and had been adapted for many purposes after the building became an institution. It offered very attractive and quite adequate facilities for a nursery school. Three playrooms, a washroom, and a small auxiliary room were established on the ground floor. Upstairs, two large rooms provided facilities for staff and volunteer activities in connection with the school. Set at one end of the large west garden, it allowed plenty of space for outdoor activity with slides, swings, sandbox, wagons, tricycles, etc. It was here, under the supervision of nursery teachers, that we hoped to provide our children with some formal group play training.

Individual play sessions in the main building were started with the children eighteen months to two years old. Gradually, all the youngsters were given daily opportunities in these sessions. As one by one they could attend to play materials for a short while and use them somewhat constructively, and as they showed signs of trusting the adults in charge, they were "graduated" to the coach-house nursery school. We continued to foster the feeling that dependable, interested adults were in charge of their lives. By keeping the number of children in a playroom restricted to two or three, the adults could give very close attention to each child, encouraging and guiding him so intensively that he would not be confused by the variety of social and intellectual stimuli in the somewhat expanded setting. Playroom time in the nursery school was limited at first to 20 or 30 minutes because even under these highly controlled circumstances the children were still distractable and erratic, and their behaviour would soon get beyond the ability of the supervisor to control. As the months went by, the play periods were prolonged, and the nursery-school time expanded to outdoor and indoor play, washing and toilet routines, and cookie, rest, and story-circle times. At no time did the full nursery-school programme exceed two hours daily for each child. Some children were able to cope with such extended play periods only two or three days a week.

The environment provided mental stimulation by presenting a selection of toys with obvious goals. The challenge was to make a simple choice, to use the play material in an appropriate way, to achieve success rapidly, and hence to experience the satisfaction of having brought something to a successful conclusion. At first the adults had to make the choices and demonstrate the use of the toys over and over again. Toys were deliberately chosen to broaden the child's concept of his world. The doll centre was provided with play equipment similar to the furnishings found in a home. Interestingly enough, the furnishings were never used appropriately until many of the children had acquired "volunteer mothers" who took them to their homes for visits and through whom the children had their first home life experiences.

A playroom routine was established which the children learned to follow. The instructions "take a toy from the shelf," "take it to a table," "sit down," "play with it," "return it to the shelf," provided a secure and constant basis for behaviour. Minimum rules regarding noise, boisterous activity, and destruction of other children's work were applied, and the children were taken from the playroom if they were unable to follow them. Gradually they seemed pleased to incorporate the rules into their frame of reference, and were proud of their ability to carry them out. Always, of course, they needed a great deal of help from adults. Very slowly, over a period of months, we were able to see an increase in self-direction and purposeful activity, as the children adapted to the new setting and became interested in the satisfaction it offered.

Two developments could be discerned. As the children became interested in the world outside themselves, their interest was reflected in an increased attention span. Further, they were able to graduate step by step from simple toys to more complex materials which demanded more skill, concentration, and imagination. Paper, paste, finger painting, and clay were used at a simple creative level. The children began to be interested in listening to stories in groups of four or five. At first, stories about very concrete experiences, such as frying an egg in a frying pan and eating it, held their attention. Later they became capable of the less concrete experience of listening to a story without active participation. Music proved soothing, and simple songs were learned and acted out. Giving children water and water toys to play with had a settling effect whenever they became too excited or over-stimulated.

Although there were wide individual differences among the children, all of them showed increasing capacity to shift from mere acceptance of adult-imposed goals regarding the use of play materials to goals which they imposed upon themselves, as they began to see the possibilities in the toys. The thrill of satisfaction was apparent in their faces as they realized that they had "made" something which they planned themselves.

In addition to an observable change in mental attitude, physical skills, through the use of both outdoor and indoor play equipment, were improving. Muscles had been underdeveloped and weak. Gradually, increasing use of tricycles, wagons, kiddy cars, slides, swings, teeter-totters, walking boards, and sand-piles for outdoor play brought about a tremendous improvement in gross muscle control. Using scissors and paint brushes, pasting, fitting puzzles, piling blocks, carrying water, passing cookies, and similar activities brought about observable improvements in fine muscle skills even within a period of months.

Although much disturbing behaviour persisted in many of the children, the observation of blossoming personalities countered any discouragement the staff might have felt. As the children began to have contacts with the community outside the institution through the agency of the "volunteer mothers," these new experiences too were integrated with opportunities offered in the nursery school and gained expression through the child's improving skills in imaginative and constructive play. The level of the children's play was constantly used as a diagnostic yardstick of their progress in overall emotional well-being.

Encouraging Emotional Well-being

Emotional well-being can arise from the sense of satisfaction which comes from playing constructively with a toy or putting forth effort to create something from play materials.

Arousing interest is the first step in this process of developing well-being. Such things as a "junk bag," containing scraps of all types and taken into the nursery wards in the evenings for the children, developed interest in exploring. Simple toys pertaining to their simplified worlds aroused curiosity. At first the adult had to be constantly present to demonstrate how to use things. Gradually, as the children developed interests within themselves, the adults could permit the children more freedom of expression. Self-initiated interest became a built-in quality, attention spans increased, self-confidence became greater. The children became happier. Choices that had baffled and confused them at first, making them anxious, later provided moments of delicious lingering in front of a variety of materials, some of which might be used for special occasions such as Christmas and Hallowe'en. Satisfactory decision-making proved a further source of self-confidence.

Another factor which furthered the development of emotional well-being was the children's acceptance of the few simple regulations established around the nursery school procedures. Rules such as "no running in the playrooms," "no destroying another child's toys," "no running up the slide," were at first imposed and enforced by adults with as simple an explanation as possible. With constant and immediate insistance that such rules be recognized, the children finally could be kept under control. If a child was disturbing the group, he was removed to play alone. Such disciplinary measures, which had meaning to the children, were sufficient to encourage them to impose controls on themselves. Gradually, the reasonableness of the rules seemed to be accepted by the children and they themselves would assume responsibility to carry them out. This transfer of outward control to inner self-control was rewarding for adults and children alike. The feeling that they were in charge of some aspects of their own lives gave the children self-confidence which was reflected in more reasonable behaviour.

Living and Playing Together

Despite the fact that the children had lived together for a large part of their lives, they were unable to relate to each other. When taken to a playroom together, they pushed and shoved, trampled and clawed each other as they might any moving object in their way. Their lack of feeling and their indifference to each other were discouraging. The immediate problem was to find a method of arousing some sensitivity in them towards each other. We hoped to do so primarily by establishing an adult-child attachment. As we worked with the children, our expectation was borne out. Once they began to develop a feeling of self-worth as a reflection of adult dependence, they turned their attention to other children. In ten months they seemed to have run the gamut from disinterested apathy to uncontrolled responsiveness. It was necessary to impose controls.

As their general excitability was carried into the playrooms and playground, the children would scream, fight, throw things, run away, and defy the adults. Therefore, we had to ensure that no more than two or three children were in a playroom at one time. The supervising staff controlled their play closely by being with them at all times to direct their attention towards the toys rather than to each other. Frequently, two staff members supervised three children. Gradually, control was regained and the children could live comfortably beside each other.

By June, 1959 (18 months after treatment began), each child remaining in the institution was having some nursery-school experience and was coping with that experience according to his own capacity. Some children remained happy and well directed with five days of nursery school each week, while other children could cope adequately with only two or three days. Four of the children showing the best progress were sent to community nursery schools where they would have the opportunity to copy the behaviour of normal children. Only one child could not cope with this experience and his behaviour became overwhelmingly aggressive.

By August, 1959, many of the children had gained valuable experience with their "volunteer mothers," and they reflected the experience in imaginative play. Conversations about life in a home, or about church, streetcars, or stores was now rooted in the children's own experience. By December, 1959, we saw the rewards of our programme when the children were seen to be capable of free play in very small groups for a short space of time.

The nursery school was used to develop physical as well as mental health. We were fully aware that an improvement in physical health would inevitably be reflected in mental well-being. Therefore a happy balance was worked out between outdoor and indoor activity, quiet and energetic play, active participation and simply watching and listening. In the summer, we took advantage of warm weather and sunshine to use the gardens for a wider variety of activity. Extra time was spent outdoors for picnics, snacks, stories, games, and discussions. The gardens were fortunately very large and attractive, with large and small trees, plants, and flower beds, in addition to the runways provided for the children's wagons, tricycles, and kiddy cars. There was plenty of space for swings, slides, and sand-piles, and lots of grass to play on. In the spring, the blossoms on the fruit trees made the gardens particularly beautiful with their gay colour and elusive perfume.

Nursery School Staff

Our success in using the nursery school therapeutically resulted in large part from our careful selection of nursery school teachers. They had been especially trained to supervise and run nursery schools for normal children. Part of their training had been in child development and psychology, which gave them a basis for understanding the behaviour, not only of normal children, but of those who deviated from the normal. Their understanding of the limitations of deprived children enabled them to lower their expectations successfully, while at the same time slowly providing constant stimulation towards normal development. Knowledge of what to expect of normal children was invaluable insofar as it gave the staff goals to which they might aim, and at the same time permitted them to accept failures with equanimity, knowing that further simplification of requirements would enable the children once more to get a foothold from which they could advance in their development.

The understanding these teachers possessed enabled them to assess each child individually, recognizing that each had his own starting point in learning, and that each would progress at his own rate. Their attitude probably played as important a part in the success of the play programme as their knowledge of appropriate toys and their special skill in the supervision and control of the children. Because the proper point of view about the children's progress was so important, the nursery school was used as a training centre, and the nursery-school staff members were regarded as training supervisors for the rest of the staff. The nursery staff was expected to complete written records at given intervals on each child in order to assess the children's development accurately.

The staff was constantly engaged in setting, evaluating, and re-setting goals for individual children and for groups. The goals pertained not only to play, but to all phases of the children's lives: sleeping, eating, dressing, dealing with adults and children, speaking, and adjusting to community experiences. The technique of evaluation was particularly useful in the nursery school where each child was judged in the same setting and by the same criteria.

By September, 1959 (18 months after the beginning), we could look upon some success. Small groups of children could play together constructively for a short time, physical and mental health were showing marked improvement, and social interaction with contemporaries was proving enjoyable. Although the play programme alone was not responsible for all this progress, it made a large contribution.

8

The Volunteers

IN RETROSPECT, it appears that much of the success of the whole plan of treatment was due to the contribution of volunteers. We had been working with the children only a short while when it became apparent that each child would benefit from a person who would be interested in him alone and to whom he could feel he "belonged." We expected that the relationship provided by a "volunteer mother" who could attach herself to one child to whom she might devote her exclusive attention would enhance the child's feeling of uniqueness and support a developing concept of self-worth. A "volunteer mother" would introduce him to new experiences in the community, and could allay his fears of a wider world.

Whoever would take on the job of being a "mother" to these unusual youngsters needed to be a person of sensitivity, understanding, and patience. She also had to be able to stick with the job as long as the child needed her, but relinquish him when his need was fulfilled. Ideally we needed a volunteer for each child, but where could we find women in such numbers and of the necessary calibre to meet our requirements? We needed people who would come consistently, once or twice a week, on whom a child could depend unquestioningly, and who could accept peculiar behaviour, expressed hostility, tears, and erratic activity. We needed people who could withstand public censure, and who could support a child without flinching when his behaviour precipitated curiosity and ridicule.

No group of such women was readily available. Furthermore, once a child started to respond to treatment by the professional staff, it became a matter of real importance that he be supported by a lay person who fully understood his particular problem and who was willing to cater to his unique needs. Therefore, any plan involving volunteer mothers would necessarily require a "matching" of mother and child to assure a minimum of friction.

One of the great weaknesses of a volunteer in any organization is inconsistency in contributing whatever service he is offering. Often such inconsistency arises from a lack of conviction that his services are essential or even vital to the organization he is helping. Since we needed dependable volunteer help a training programme was started with the aim of imparting our conviction that the children needed one consistent person in their lives. The programme was open only to women who stated their willingness either to spend at least half a day a week with some youngster or to drive children to clinics, hospitals, church, and stores. To those unable to devote themselves to a child, a variety of other duties were open, such as sewing, mending and painting toys, knitting, or office work. However, the bulk of the duties involved working directly with the children.

The training period lasted for six weeks, the first three weekly sessions being devoted to recording observations of the children's behaviour. The children's reactions to adults were noted particularly, and were later discussed with senior staff members who attempted to interpret the significance of the behaviour. The last three sessions were devoted to formal lectures and discussions of child development. The ways in which these institutionalized children deviated from normal were pointed up, emphasis being placed on their lack of ability to form relationships with either adults or children. We stressed that a volunteer could create a relationship in a child's life which no one else could do.

Once the preliminary course was over, each volunteer was assigned a special child. An attempt was made to match the two to create a harmonious relationship. By matching a child with a volunteer who was able to accept his particular personality and cater to his unique needs, we promoted the child's greatest progress. The least-deprived youngsters were the first to be assigned. In addition, a special group of volunteers was trained in nursery-school procedures, and this group assisted the nursery school staff.

Sometimes we were able to make use of the neurotic needs of volunteers (normally regarded as deficits), and were able to turn them into assets in dealing with certain children. For example, a childless woman with deep unsatisfied needs to "mother" could contribute greatly to the first stage of a child's recovery. She could foster the necessary intense dependency that gives the initial boost to the first step in his emotional development. Later, conflict would arise when the child was ready to take some self-initiated action which moved him away from her attachment. The more he would demonstrate signs of emotional health by attempting to make decisions of his own, the less this kind of woman would be able to meet his changing needs. Finally, unable to permit him to grow beyond her dependency, she would actually mitigate his recovery by fighting his developing personality. At this point, the child had to be transferred either to a foster or adopting mother or to another volunteer who could enjoy the child's initiative and who could tolerate some degree of non-conformity. The procedure was very hard on the few volunteers who were "used" this way. The decision to place a volunteer and child in such a tenuous position gave us many days of worry. However, concern for the children usually outweighed our concern for a volunteer, particularly in the first stages of the treatment programme when we needed many extra people. Fortunately, after all the children had been placed in homes, only one long-term unresolved emotional conflict remained, that of a neurotic unmarried woman who had lived alone for many years beside the institution. She had watched the children during their years of tenure and when the treatment programme started, offered her services as a volunteer. Long after "her child" had been placed in an adoption home she complained about the quality of the new parents and the unsuitability of his surroundings. She constantly demanded to visit "her child."

The success of the volunteer programme could be measured in months. By April of the first year of treatment (4 months after the beginning of the programme) many of the volunteers were well settled with children, and a mutually rewarding relationship was building up. The least seriously disturbed youngsters welcomed the visits to various places in the community with curiosity. When the visits were continued week after week, their curiosity was replaced by enthusiasm and anticipation of the next visit. They looked forward to seeing the volunteers each week. By June, there seemed to be a decided improvement in the children's speech. They were fumbling for words to express their interest in their new experiences. Development of facility in speech encouraged conversation among those children still without volunteers.

As the number of children receiving treatment was reduced by adoption, by foster placement, or by return to their own homes, more professional attention could be given to the more disturbed youngsters remaining. When they responded to this more intensive effort, they too were matched with a volunteer mother. In a few cases, it was not possible to make a suitable match between volunteer and child. Concentrated attention from the professional staff seemed the only appropriate treatment for the children who were deeply disturbed as well as deprived. For example, intensely hostile children might prove hazardous should their aggression be released against a volunteer who could not tolerate it. Such a situation would not only be detrimental to any gains made in therapy but might pose a threat in the future to any possibility of forming a relationship with a foster or adopting mother.

Those disturbed children who were placed with volunteers proved a challenge to the patience and understanding of the most sensitive persons. At first, some of them resisted being taken beyond the doors of the institution by screaming, kicking, and throwing themselves to the floor. Others showed their discomfort by withdrawal from their volunteer mother for many weeks before accepting her care. As volunteers became a part of the organization, those children without a "mother" talked freely about the time when they would have one, trusting implicitly that their turn would come. And indeed, with very few exceptions their time did come. Those few who could not be suitably matched with a volunteer were placed in foster or adoptive care without any intervening link between professional help in the institution and life in a home.

One feature of the volunteer programme, after it was well under way, was weekend visits in a volunteer's home. This introduction to family life, while broadening the children's experiences, worried the staff lest it might make the contrast between life in the institution and life in a home too sharp for a child who yearned for a home of his own. It brought a whole new perspective to his life; the place of a father in a child's world, what a mother does at home, how people slept, ate, shopped, had cars repaired, shovelled snow, cut grass, and paid bills. In order to lead up to these experiences, storytimes, nursery-school games, and conversation times were used as introductory measures. There were a variety of reactions from the children on the first visits. Some were fearful and wanted to return "home" to the institution at bed time. Some seemed content, but tense while visiting, and were obviously relieved to come back to the institution on Monday morning. Later in the same day they might develop sufficient courage to boast of their experiences to the other children. As the visits were repeated and the children became more integrated into the volunteer family, they were more and more reluctant to return to the institution at the end of the visit. On the whole, we considered these weekend visits to be valuable introductions to family life, helping prepare the way for a final placement. One of the most beneficial outcomes was the compatibility which developed between some of the children and the volunteer families, resulting in three adoptions and one foster placement into the volunteers' homes.

As the treatment programme took shape over the first few months, gradually the volunteer section became a unit of the total plan. It included not only the volunteer "mothers," but also a great variety of other people with important but not so essential duties. One important job which was also a considerable nuisance to the staff was keeping the toys painted and in good repair. The skills of the staff members were needed with the children, and we objected to their using their energies repairing toys. Volunteer workshops were organized to take care of these duties whenever a "repairing bee" seemed to be needed.

The evening period between supper time and bed time was always a most difficult one. The children would be weary and excitable and the energy of the staff would be wearing thin. Toy-carts, looked after by volunteers, greatly relieved the pressure on the staff, easing tension at bedtime. Additional services, such as driving children to hospital clinics, staying with them for examination, sewing dresses and night-gowns for the girls, and knitting for the boys, were provided by the volunteers. A pianist volunteered each day to provide music for the song circles in the nursery school. Twenty students from the University of Toronto made up a crew of painters and repairmen to do odd jobs around the building and help keep the toys in good shape. Two psychology students from the University helped care for the children for a few hours each week.

By the end of March, three months after the inception of the volunteer programme, 80 women were involved in the organization and obligated to carry out some consistent duty. A volunteer headed the administration of these activities and looked after the necessary clerical work. This was a full-time job in itself, for it involved making numerous appointments for shopping, outings, and visits to hospitals and clinics, establishing times for children to be in and out, arranging for emergencies when a driver was sick, encouraging volunteers to keep written records about their contact with the children, and generally making sure that the whole programme functioned smoothly.

By May the number of children in the care of the McNeil Home began to decrease and no further volunteer mothers were needed. In fact, we began to accumulate a list of "extra" people and could more and more make a careful selection of the persons best suited to look after particular children. By this time every child was benefiting in some degree from contact with a volunteer "mother."

As the treatment programme drew towards completion, and the

"family" plan, with units of three, four, or five children, was set up with one staff member (called a "unit mother") in charge of each unit, the character of the volunteer help was modified. Instead of a volunteer for each child, there were now one or two volunteers for each unit. Each volunteer was concerned with several children, rather than only one, as had formerly been the case. She would visit with them for a day, take one or two out shopping or for some special activity, and generally make herself useful to the children and liked by them. The change was made to avoid any threat to the relationship between the unit mother and her children. Gradually, as the children moved to foster and adoptive homes, the need for volunteers disappeared.

At first, considerable work had been demanded from the staff to organize the volunteer group and introduce it to the aims of treatment. In the long run, the programme lightened the load of the staff while providing for the children invaluable emotional support and opportunities to experience somewhat normal ways of living in the community. Written records, in addition to providing needed orientation and training, seemed also to make a valuable contribution to the volunteers' understanding of the needs of children. (See the appendix for samples of the records and a bulletin issued for volunteers in May, 1959.) Bolstered by the continuous support of the regular staff, the volunteers added greatly to the institution's effort to develop and strengthen the children's feelings of personal well-being.

9

Progress

THE TREATMENT PROGRAMME was initiated by people sufficiently concerned with research to want to record accurately what happened to the children in response to whatever steps were taken to help them. To this end, they periodically recorded behaviour in "Security Records."* In addition, a daily diary was kept by the supervisor about every aspect of the centre. Each staff member was instructed to record any unusual incident and any significant response of the children to her care. Records were kept by the building administrator, who was also the dietician in charge of the children's meals. Each division head was expected to produce a monthly report of the progress or changes which came under her jurisdiction.

As a result, monthly reports of the running of the institution provided a record of successes, disappointments, set-backs, and the warmth of a complex accumulation of people, assembled for one purpose—the rehabilitation of deprived youngsters. Happily, these records reflected many of the incidental human concerns which are lost when the total work is reported. The following report was written one year after the programme had been started. In retrospect, we know it reflects undue optimism about the degree of recovery of the children. But this optimism kept the staff going and had developed in response to a real change for the better.

Neil McNeil Infants' Home
Monthly Report

December, 1958
Number of Children: 49

The month of December ended a most interesting and challenging year for staff and one of tremendous growth and development for the children of Neil McNeil. The greatest reward was to see two of the older damaged

*See appendix.

children develop into apparently well youngsters and leave Neil McNeil, one to adoptive parents, the other to foster home placement. [See case histories in the five following chapters.]

The month was one of stirring excitement. The older children (three- and four-year-olds) anticipated Christmas—the birthday of Baby Jesus (birthdays and babies having real meanings). They would come home from nursery school singing "Jingle Bells" and very proud of bringing home their work, which took the form of pictures pasted on paper plates or coloured paper, paper chains, and Christmas bows. Daily the children appeared more sociable and over-talkative, although speech was still very jerky and erratic.

As was stated last month, the home is now able to function within a more relaxed structured programme. The fewer children there are, the more individual care the staff can give them. The last two months has shown a more general acceleration in the children's well-being in spite of considerable increases in colds and minor illnesses. The new environment with fewer pressures on staff and children has shown many heartening effects on the older children (three and four years of age). The following are casual observations of some of the units.

General Approach to New Situations

Seating arrangements were changed in dining rooms in order to prevent over-stimulating social interaction among the children at meals. Immediately behaviour problems decreased and the children accepted the change and appeared to understand its purpose.

Three younger children, aged two to three, who were ready to eat in dining room, were introduced to this more controlled setting. They anticipated the change and enjoyed the move. Charlie, 2 years and ten months, and Linda, two years and eight months, conformed immediately. Margaret, a difficult child who has many problems in social relationships, responded negatively for a few days. Two months ago these children would have found the change very disturbing. They still sleep and play in their own unit.

Three months ago, many children feared changes; new experiences were traumatic. Now they approach life with enthusiasm.

Adult beds were introduced. Six months ago such a foreign piece of furniture would have been used destructively (pushed, jumped on, but not slept on), now a large bed is a sign of great prestige and all are asking when will they be "big enough." One year ago a crib represented their secure world.

The strange and awesome figure of Santa Claus appeared abruptly on the scene one afternoon. Only three children out of fifty refused to accept him and his gifts.

The social interaction between staff and children is becoming a joy, especially now that language is showing improvement. "Una, you be sick and I'll be doctor. Lie down on this bed, Una," says Joseph to his unit mother. All five children in the unit participated in game for ten minutes. "Ah, poor Charlie, are you sick?" says Linda, aged two years nine months, as she goes to his bed and pats him.

When sick children are not seriously ill they are now kept in their rooms. Often one sees the other children going on little errands for them. Paul was seen getting out of bed, going to the sink and filling a glass of water for Gregory, who was too miserable to get up. These two children had been left alone in their room when this incident took place.

The children are allowed to play in playrooms or their bedrooms when not expected to conform to routines.

"Where are you going, Patrick?"

"Oh, just for a little visit to see Johnny," he replied as he marched down the hall to Johnny's unit.

The common usage of "Mummy" for all female adults is still heard, but more frequently every day one hears a child ask, "What's her name?" Verbal identification of themselves, their peers, and adults is increasing.

The bed-time hours for the children upstairs are becoming a much happier, relaxed time. As the children are taking more responsibility for dressing, undressing, and using the toilet, more time is left for free play (sharing toys with each other, taking turns in a wheelbarrow) and for individual help or story time with the unit mother. The unit mothers are given the responsibility of buying their own play materials and decorating their own units, a responsibility resulting in individuality, pride in their units, and more interest in the welfare and development of "their children." One can observe the youngsters sitting around the table while unit mother Chris builds a house with "mini-bricks" and Johnny makes a road for David to drive his car up to Chris's house. Unit mother Theresa brought in two old magazines. Her tired little ones are swarming around her while she cuts out cars for them to paste as pictures.

Plans are being made to revise schedules after the New Year to improve the toddler and infant units. As the children's needs are changing and they are demanding more from their world, it is apparent that the staff needs more help in understanding pre-school development. It is anticipated that five children will be leaving Neil McNeil Home in January, thus allowing for smaller units downstairs and making space for another playroom.

During December many children remained indoors with colds. It was very rewarding to observe children in small groups playing well with equipment. They played happily in bed with toys and could be left alone for short intervals. At no time, even among the overly-aggressive two-year-olds, was there confusion. Gradually, less aimless activity is seen.

Every child now eagerly awaits his outings in the community. Five months ago, only a selected few could tolerate anything more than a ride in the pram or a walk in the park. Since October, weekend visits to homes are increasing. On December 18, twelve children were out overnight with volunteers and twenty were out for the day.

December 25—Christmas

One case of measles was discovered on December 16. All the children were classed as contacts, but were permitted to go to homes of adults, or to homes where the children had already had the disease. On December 24, fourteen children went home overnight with volunteers. In the morning the remaining thirty-eight found their socks full of bananas, lollypops, and toys at the foot of their beds. By 10:30, all but five children were out for the day. Many loyal staff members took children home. At 5:30 the children "drifted" back home, happy, tired, and content to fall asleep at 6:30 with the new public address system (a gift from a volunteer) softly playing Brahms' lullaby.

Only one of the children had been brought home early by the staff as a result of over-excitability. Another child with a normal temperature had a stomach upset. He was brought home by volunteer.

Volunteers

On December 13, a nursery school tea was held for volunteers. About ten of the better-adjusted children were allowed to roam about and pass cookies and enjoy the fun. They were pleased to be dressed up and clung to their volunteer mothers, proud to have "their" lady coming to the tea party. The children are quite aware of their own and other children's volunteers. They are possessive and feel it is their right to have a family in the outside world. Many children are reasoning, are talking about their weekends, and, if they have not been out, say they are going soon. The staff never ceases to be amazed at this miraculous development.

Report of the Neil McNeil Nursery School

Plans are well under way for Christmas. A greater variety of creative materials are being introduced: bright tinfoils, Christmas shapes, Christmas trees, chains, decorated paper plates, Christmas stockings and hats.

The children have become overly excited by their activities together and must be slowed down again. They are showing encouraging improvement in their ability to reason and to see relationships. They are enjoying music periods three times weekly and are learning Christmas songs and hearing Christmas stories. The children are showing sufficient self-control to go from the music circle to ask a teacher in the hall for a plate of cookies which they take back and pass around the group before serving themselves. Two months previously, they would have devoured the cookies so no one else could get them.

The following is a partial list of the children who have been in nursery school this last year.

Patrick, 4 years, attends morning nursery school five days a week. The last two months have seen a decidedly happy change in this child. He likes music periods, enjoys singing. Enjoys creative work and toys. Very mischievous and teasing. Talks well, has a very inquiring mind. Has an excellent unit mother, sometimes acts up at school, especially in playground, so he can go home to her. Pat was one of the older disturbed children who started with individual attention in the spring, then proceeded to a small afternoon group. He was doing so well, he was sent to outside nursery school where he slowly regressed. Returned to our nursery school in July where he was given much help. Once again he is becoming established, happy, and affectionate. Occasionally he sucks his thumb and withdraws from the group, especially if disciplined or not permitted to have his own way.

Sheila, 4 years, 3 months, attends nursery school five days a week. Began receiving individual play therapy in the spring. At this time, she had a bad rash which she scratched until it bled, owing to an emotional upset. With much help in the playroom, she has calmed down and begun to trust adults and enjoy toys. She had to be watched very closely at first and kept in the smaller playroom to keep her from becoming over-stimulated. Now she enjoys the larger playrooms and scratches very little. She likes to boss and direct the other children—wants to do everything herself. She enjoys the doll centre, washing dishes, talking to dolls, bathing them. She can be difficult to manage; she plays for adult attention, and sometimes has to be removed from the group. She is happy at school.

Wayne, 3 years, 11 months, is an older damaged child who began with individual play therapy and then moved to the small afternoon group. In July he came into the morning school five days a week. He plays well with toys and creative material. Enjoys both music and story circles. He used to whine constantly and would use only one word, now carries on a happy conversation. He is now attending outside nursery school where he is adjusting very well. This boy has wonderful volunteer parents who have helped him a great deal. All his outside experiences are now played out in the nursery.

Janice, 4 years, 2 months, began her nursery school experiences with individual guidance and therapy; then proceeded to a small afternoon group. This youngster has extremely poor eyesight and until being fitted for glasses a few months ago had to put things a few inches from her face to see them. This, needless to say, made her very frustrated, unhappy, and solemn. In July she began morning school. Later she wore glasses which took her some time to adjust to, but when she had mastered them, her whole personality changed. She now laughs, teases, and enjoys this new world she sees. We have had to limit her to every other day at school as we found every day proved more exciting than she could manage happily. Her play isn't as good or constructive as that of many of the other children, but considering her first great handicap, she is adjusting quite well. Plays well in doll centre and with simple toys.

Michael, 3 years, 6 months, began individual play therapy in the spring, then came to morning nursery school five days a week. This child has a limp as a result of polio. He has frequent temper tantrums, throwing himself on the ground and kicking at the slightest provocation. Many indirect controls are being used, and he is beginning to accept adult guidance. His interest span with toys is short and he needs help to increase it. He was sick, off and on, for a week or two, and began to regress. He had so many tantrums that he had to be taken out of school and sent back to individual play sessions. He is coming along nicely once again.

Linda, 3 years, 3 months, is a withdrawn girl with many hidden fears. She began last spring with individual play therapy, then went on to morning school in July, five days a week. At this time she hardly spoke a word and had a great fear of men. She just watched everything from a distance. Now she is talkative, friendly, plays well, notices anything new about her and remarks on it. Once a solemn child, there is now a ready shy smile and twinkle in her eye. She still has many fears of the world outside the institution, but her twice-a-week volunteer mother is doing a great deal to help her outgrow these troubles.

Rodney, 3 years, 10 months, is a troubled, sensitive child, who began with individual play therapy in the spring and then went into a small afternoon group. In July, he came to morning school five days a week. During this time, he has changed from a very aggressive child who had temper tantrums, bit, and fought a great deal, and who was frightened of men, to a child who has many controls within himself. He is talking well, is constructive and imaginative in play. He enjoys teasing and is noisy; there is a twinkle in his eye, and he has a shy smile. He still has fears (men), and some tantrums, but he has come a long way on the road to recovery.

Garry, 3 years, 9 months, is a quiet, sober boy who began with individual play therapy, then came into the morning school in July, five days a week. Like the other children, he had little or no speech. Now, though still shy, he talks, observes things around him, teases, and is beginning to be noisy. He enjoys the other children, is kind by nature, and has a slow winning smile. He is enjoying creative work. He needs more outside community experience and is going into a home.

Philip, 3 years, 4 months, is a withdrawn boy whose chief comfort in life has been eating. Began with individual play therapy in the spring, and in July came to morning school five days a week. Philip always conformed so much in the playroom, playing very quietly with a toy, that is was easy to neglect him for the more demanding child. We began praising his work a great deal, repeating words and sentences to encourage speech, for he did not even speak single words. His outside play was lethargic. The last two months have seen a great change in him, as he is playing well, is noisy, and teases. He is doing things to attract the teacher's attention and is fighting for his own way. His speech is still slow but he can talk now. There is often a mischievous twinkle in his eyes. He is much happier within himself.

James, 3 years, 7 months, the boy with the sagging mouth and constant drool, with a whine instead of speech. He began play therapy in the spring at which time he was taking treatments for his lame arm, the aftermath of polio. In July, he began morning school five days a week. He needed much reassurance to approach each new toy. Now he plays constructively with toys and enjoys creative work and music and story circles. He has become overly sensitive to people and so demanding (talking at great length, arguing with the teacher) that he sometimes has to be removed from playroom until he quiets down. It is felt Jamie is ready to try a community nursery school in January, 1959.

Ann, 3 years, 3 months, has dark moods and constant intense temper tantrums. The corners of her mouth were always down. She began with individual play therapy in the spring, then morning school in July, five days a week. In the beginning, there was no speech, just sounds. When she wanted a toy, she would touch the teacher, point to the toy on a shelf and then to herself. On being assured she could play with the toy, she would take it from the shelf but when through with it, would go through the pointing and grunting to have it put back. The teacher would name the toys, using single words as much as possible. Gradually, Ann began using words, and then sentences. She became much more secure. There are many smiles and laughter now and she enjoys other children. A setback came when she was changed to a new room with a new unit mother; her moods and tantrums returned. School was cut to every other day, and more individual help and reassurance was given to her. Now, she has returned to her happier self. Ann has left us to go into a good foster home.

John, 3 years, 9 months, a little boy with a bad habit of rubbing his neck until red and sucking his tongue at the same time. He had intensive individual play therapy in the spring, and improved greatly. In July, he began the morning school, five days a week. His whole appearance seemed to change as he learned inner controls. He played constructively with toys, had a good interest span, and was imaginative, enjoying creative work and story and music circles. He changed from a withdrawn, silent child to a communicative, social one. He was started in a community nursery school which he attended for about two months, but things became too much for him and he regressed. He was brought back to our school in a much disturbed state—biting and scratching. He seemed glad to be back. He started in a small group and now is in a larger one. He has been coming along nicely in the last week. A good unit mother is helping him too.

George, 4 years, 2 months, was one of the very badly damaged children put in a special unit with two other damaged children. At first uncommunicative and timid, he began nursery school by coming to the playground for a short time each day in September. His unit mother stayed with him, then little by little left him alone. When he felt secure in the playground, he came into the schoolroom setting for a short time each day. He began in the small playroom to make it easier to handle the controls, direct and indirect, and then moved into the larger playroom where he stayed the full time. School five days a week was an exciting experience for him. He is playing well with toys and enjoying creative work. At first he was solemn and talked very little. Now he talks well, smiles and laughs, and loves to tease his teachers. He has reached a point of needing more outside experiences and contacts. He will begin the new year in a community nursery school.

Charlie, 3 years, is a quiet, small-boned child who began with individual play therapy in the spring and joined the junior group held in the afternoon, starting in July. About September, we tried him with the morning group of older children but he wasn't ready as he was afraid of the older children, so he went back to the junior group where his play was good, though his interest span was short. He likes to paste and paint and to taste things. Has just been promoted to the morning school and is attending every other day until he is well adjusted. This time he is doing quite well.

While still quiet by nature, he now talks fairly well, and loves to tease the adults. He needs much more adult guidance.

Mary, 3 years, was a troubled child who began with individual play therapy last spring, and then joined a small group of juniors at afternoon school. Her play habits varied with her moods, which were often dark and hostile. She attended school every other day, as attendance every day proved too much for her to handle. She has moved on to the morning group with older children, but is still attending only every other day. At the moment, Mary lives with a group of children much younger than herself whose baby ways she copies. Soon she will be moved to an older group. There are many smiles these days, with plenty of teasing. She still needs a great deal of help, but has come a long way.

Joanne, 3 years, 2 months, had individual play therapy in the spring, and began junior school in August. She was very quiet in the beginning and would sit for a long time holding a doll, sometimes making sounds. She has always liked dolls and plays in the doll centre for a long time; it is her chief interest. She now uses short sentences, and has a deep voice and laughter. Very simple toys can be constructively used. She is interested in the story or music circle. She attends school every other day.

Maintenance—Housekeeping—Food Services

Above areas appear to be operating as smoothly as possible under present conditions.

Maintenance. General repairs are constant in all areas.

1. Shed has now been built for outdoor play equipment, which will be erected on grounds as soon as possible.

2. Bathtub has now been installed in second-floor bathroom, and bathroom has been redecorated (plastered, etc.) by handyman.

3. All observation windows are now inserted where required.

4. Drains continue to be choked occasionally, and taps continue to drip despite frequent renewal of washers.

5. It has been necessary to call service department rather frequently to repair the first-floor kitchen refrigerator, which functions occasionally.

6. Now almost every door in the building has a high handle, reflecting the growth and activities of children. Likewise several nursery gates have been changed—higher and more solid hooks.

7. Three new electric heaters have been bought, for use throughout building. (Basement playroom has no radiator and several of the nurseries are very draughty.)

8. A gate has been placed at the bottom of the stairway leading to infirmary, as there are several toddlers around this area who delight in climbing the stairs, which are rather steep.

Staff

1. Several members have been sick in the past two months.

2. Two bedrooms on third floor which were occupied by the house mother and night nurse are now used as rest rooms for staff on split duty, etc.

3. New polisher is required by housecleaning staff.

Children. The majority have now a good appetite.

1. There has been a slight change in dining room routine. Groups are now much smaller per table, thus more direct supervision can be given.

2. Chicken is now being served, and within the next month several new dishes will be introduced.

3. It is hoped that soon the older children will accept paper serviettes rather than bibs. Soon it should also be possible for a plate of bread and butter to be placed on each table without each child grabbing for it. Presently, it is served at the main serving table.

4. In several nurseries a bed has been placed to accustom a child to it in preparation for his placement in a home.

The overall picture is remarkably different from that of a year ago.

Important—The building deteriorates daily, pipes burst, sinks are condemned, refrigerators and stoves do not function properly. (Several ovens cannot be used and are beyond repair.)

INFIRMARY REPORT FOR DECEMBER, 1958

Date	Patient	Temperature (°F)	Ailment and treatment
Dec. 8	O. D.	103.2	Chest cold. *Im.*: Achromycin.
" 9	P. M.	103.2	Cold—responded to symptomatic treatment.
" 10	J. D.	103.3	Chest cough—treated symptomatically
" 11	G. P.	98.6	Vomited seven times.
" 12	R. D.	104.3	Chest cold.
" 12	C. C.	103	Chest cold.
" 14	M. O.	104	Chronic chest cold.
" 14	J. G.	105	Virus. *Im.*: Penicillin.
" 15	R. B.	104	Chest cold. *Im.*: Achromycin.
" 16	R. Mc.	101	Convulsed at 2:30, treated with Phenobarbitol.
" 17	P. R.	—	Measles.
" 18	P. M.	104.2	Cold. *Im.*: Achromycin, 1 tsp. *qid*.
" 22	R. Mc.	103	Cold. Convulsed at 11 A.M.
" 22	M. W.	103	Influenza.
" 25	L. C.	102.4	Vomited twice.
" 29	D. C.	—	Measles.
" 29	J. W.	—	Measles.
" 29	L. C.	—	Measles.
" 31	A. C.	103.4	Measles. Felt very listless. *Im.*: Penicillin.
" 31	R. B.	105	Measles. *Im.*: Penicillin.
" 31	M. C.	—	Measles.
" 31	A. F.	—	Measles.
" 31	C. V.	—	Measles.

CLINICS ATTENDED AT HOSPITAL FOR SICK CHILDREN, 1958

Dec.	1	L. K.	Medical Clinic
"	2	A. D.	Neurological Clinic
"	3	R. Mc.	Psychological Clinic
"	4	O. D.	Ear, nose and throat
"	10	R. Mc.	Psychological Clinic
"	11	O. D.	Ear, nose and throat
"	11	G. P.	Eye Clinic
"	13	L. K.	Allergy Clinic

EMERGENCY AT HOSPITAL FOR SICK CHILDREN

Dec. 15	J. N.	Scalp wound—sutured.
" 31	D. E.	Severe epistaxis—cauterized and plugged.

PART THREE • THE REWARDS

The following five chapters devoted to case histories demonstrate the results of applying the principles of mental health to the rehabilitation of emotionally undeveloped or damaged children. As we worked with these widely different children, it became apparent that not all of them could be described as "damaged" but rather could more aptly be labelled "immature" or "undeveloped." Owing to the lack of normal environmental stimuli, many of them showed distorted behaviour when compared with children reared in normal homes. Their slower development was not as serious as in some children whose bizarre behaviour indicated more serious damage. Unfortunately however, they did not respond totally to the application of normal stimuli. Considerable unevenness in various aspects of their development (social, emotional, motor, intellectual) continued even after treatment and left them with somewhat unusual though not abnormal personalities. In many instances, the treatment programme brought the children to a stage where it was judged that a home setting was the only way to complete their rehabilitation.

At first all the children were treated in groups according to very broad classifications of immaturity. Sweeping environmental changes were made throughout the institution as the only means of approaching an overwhelming problem. Individual differences could not even be considered in the first general shuffle which initiated the programme. Gradually, personalities emerged from the group, according to their unique responses to the general programme. In some instances the programme in itself met enough of a child's need to initiate an improvement in his mental health. In some cases it failed to benefit a child, and special consideration had to be given to his individual needs.

The names of the five children selected for discussion in the next five chapters are fictitious. The children represent different personalities and their responses to therapy. They further demonstrate the necessity of special consideration for individual needs. The histories point up the value of following a child's progress in a systematic way and providing a frame of reference for staff discussions which lead to further treatment. They also point up the necessity to adapt and apply a variety of techniques outside the defined programme in order to bring about improvement in individual children.

Regarding the scores of the Infant Security and Pre-school Mental Health Assessment Scales shown at the beginning of each case history, it should be noted that some of the earlier scores obtained when the children were first assessed within the institution are unduly high. There are two reasons for this. First, the staff was unfamiliar with the children and could give only a superficial assessment. Second, the items indicating healthy dependence can be interpreted as passive acceptance of adult care, and in fact may describe some of the unhealthy passive states characteristic of many of the institutionalized children. Only when the quality of the behaviour was investigated more thoroughly did a truer picture emerge which was not reflected in the raw scores.

10

Gary

Age	Score (Pre-school Mental Health Assessment Form)
2 years 10 months	8
3 years 1 month	35
3 years 6 months	31
3 years 8 months	20
3 years 11 months	34
4 years 3 months	33
4 years 5 months	40

THE CHILDREN under treatment who provided the staff with the greatest surprises were those who had at first seemed to be enveloped in apathy. These were the children who fitted the classic description of maternal deprivation and about whom one could believe deprivation damage would be permanent. When first observed they seemed to be totally lacking interest in each other. They demonstrated no warmth towards adults; in fact, they seemed to anticipate nothing comforting or interesting from adults, but merely to accept them as an inevitable part of the surroundings. These children showed little initiative to move towards a toy or to take any responsibility for washing or dressing themselves. They seemed bereft of any aggressiveness and were bland and listless. When given directions they were submissive, apparently indifferent to their own welfare, and incapable of showing any rebellion.

Gary was one of these children. One staff member remembered him as withdrawn and listless at the age of ten months. He had lived in a confined environment since he was four weeks old, and until two and one half years of age his only changes of environment had consisted of occasionally being transferred from one nursery to another and, during the summer months, being placed for a few hours daily in a garden playpen. He sat passively wherever he was placed, seemingly unaware of whatever life was going on around him. By two years of age, he had developed the habit of rocking from foot to foot.

An example of his reaction to even a slight change was recorded by a staff member trained in child development. When Gary was two years and two months of age, she attempted to broaden the scope of his experience. He was taken from his nursery to a downstairs toy room.

He was tense and fearful of the stairs, even when being carried. In the playroom, he remained clinging to the adult. He smiled with delight at a soft toy rabbit. After a short time, he played on the floor, awkward, tense, and dropping things. He became very anxious and was aware of noises caused by the wind, by other children outside, and by adults on the other side of the doors. In the unfamiliar room, he began flitting aimlessly about, touching chairs, stools, and equipment. He was interested for a very short time in toy boxes, and seemed quick to learn on which shelves the boxes were placed. When it was time for him to return to the nursery, he became anxious and confused and refused the adult's help.

Gary was two years and eight months of age when the treatment programme began, and he was soon living in a setting which, although inadequate to give individual attention to each child, at least more closely met his developmental needs. His reaction to the change of programme indicated that he was anxious and insecure. Obviously he needed far more individual attention than he was getting, even under the changed programme.

Although the general tenor of his personality was listless and his relationship to others was apathetic, there were indications that he had intense feelings which occasionally came to the surface. These symptoms were not apparent to the adults working with him daily, but they were revealed by the mental health record form. He was capable of occasional bursts of aggression towards the other children, maintaining his rights and being irritable and unpleasant towards them. His lack of trust in the judgement of adults was apparent in his refusals to accept the rules of the playroom and playground. He would scream, cry, and even have temper tantrums when these rules were enforced. His inability to accept adult controls was further demonstrated at bed time, when he sometimes had tantrums, got out of bed and ran away from the adults.

By the time Gary was three years old, his general state of well-being showed improvement. It was now possible for the nursery school teachers to give him a period of time each day when he could be the only child in the playroom. They were able both to show him how to use the toys and to direct his play. Through this contact, he began to respond positively to adults. He was still generally apathetic towards the other children, however, and was quite distractable in his play. He had developed some interest in the indoor play equipment, but his concentration span was very short for his age. His large muscle control was clumsy and weak, so he remained apathetic and listless in his use of the outdoor equipment.

When he was three years and two months old, the salutary experiences of his environment were reinforced by the introduction of a volunteer mother. Judging by his Mental Health Record, he was developing closer relationships with adults; some faith in them apparently was being established. He was now accepting rules and requirements on the playground, in the playroom, and at bed time. He was eating well and showing an interest in dressing and using the toilet by himself. He no longer remained upset when hurt, as he had previously, but could permit himself to be comforted and consoled by an adult.

Within the next two months, life improved for Gary. Summer weather permitted more healthful outdoor living. There was a reduction in the number of children in the care of the institution, and therefore each child received more individual attention from the staff. Gary was moved to a unit of only ten children, and he now slept in a room with four other children. Whereas formerly he had seemed overwhelmed by large numbers of children around him, now he seemed able to enjoy the company of some of his contemporaries, as if he felt more sure of himself. He still was described as "timid" and his speech, although improving, was limited mainly to single words and occasional short sentences. There were signs that he was feeling a sense of "belonging" with his group. He would dawdle and play over his meals because he enjoyed talking to the other children.

Second Phase of Treatment

Ten months after the beginning of treatment, Gary, now three years, four months of age, was seen by the staff as being still over-conforming and timid, but as showing positive signs of a stronger personality. He was described as "friendly and affectionate" and "popular with other children." Although lacking the courage to ask for adult attention, he blossomed whenever it was received. If corrected, he became flushed with self-consciousness and was upset. He was very proud of his new-found skills with indoor play equipment, although his interest in outdoor play was still limited to rather slow and listless performance.

Gary's experience with his volunteer mother seemed to be lending him some self-confidence. He had not been with her for any long periods of time such as overnight or weekend visits; rather, she took him mainly for short excursions into the community. Gradually he became familiar with buses, large stores, animals, church, etc. Six months after their relationship had begun, when he was three years and eight months of age, marked progress could be noted. Whereas his first trips had been preceded each time with fear about new things, he gradually began to look forward with excitement to the visits of the volunteer. He enjoyed her companionship and wanted to go out "when my lady comes." He began to enjoy trips on streetcars and buses. Although still apprehensive of animals, he showed an interest in people, occasionally even approaching and talking to strangers. His curiosity about strange things overrode his initial fears, and he would handle and examine objects in department stores, admiring and replacing them without wanting to have them. Escalators were more thrilling than toys. Sometimes crowds were challenging rather than terrifying. An excursion to a barber shop for a haircut was a pleasurable adventure. He was intrigued by the church on the corner near the home and insisted on visiting it each day on first going out. He was attempting to discuss his experiences in short sentences.

Eleven months after treatment began, a visit to the home of one of Gary's trusted staff members provided the setting for his overcoming his long-standing fear of dogs. Here he was able to feed with his hands the big, black family pet. Gary patted him, and finally even went looking for him. "Doggie won't bite," was repeated with reassuring frequency.

By the time Gary was three years and eight months of age, he seemed to be emerging from quiet passivity to an enjoyment of teasing and ignoring direction; he could express his strongest feelings by having a temper tantrum. His rebellion against direction was met with jubilation by the staff, as it seemed to indicate that he was developing sufficient confidence to assert his own feelings despite the wishes of the supervising adults.

He expressed dislikes for certain foods, and he made unnecessary demands on the staff for assistance when dressing himself. His feelings were deeply hurt when he was corrected, and if hurt physically he sought out an adult for more reassurance than seemed necessary. It was at this time that he received his first discipline at nursery school, when he was taken out of the playroom because of aggressive behaviour. While playing with toys, both in the nursery section and in the residence section, he was much more self-contained than previously, and could amuse himself in constructive play. His general attitude towards his world showed a developing reasonableness. He was frequently capable of accepting explanations, and he felt important when given praise and encouragement.

Third Phase of Treatment

As the months passed, Gary continued to develop under the understanding care of interested adults. When he was four years old, he made a fine adjustment to the new family plan of care. Far from reacting with apprehension and timidity, he settled in comfortably. He was now living in a group of ten children ranging in age from twenty-two months to four and a half years of age, and he slept in a room with three children younger than himself. He and another boy were the oldest in this unit and they became great friends, showing solicitous feelings towards the babies in their unit. Gary took particular delight in "mothering" one of the youngest children, dressing and feeding her tenderly. He no longer referred to adults for help in defending himself against the other children; he could now assert himself.

Gary seemed now to be generally a happy boy, curious about his expanding world. Although timid and sensitive, he seemed at last to have put his trust in the adults around him to take care of his wants and needs. So much did he seem to be developing under the treatment programme that he was deemed ready for a new and larger experience to broaden his life beyond the highly sheltered confines of the institution.

One staff member took him to Peterborough (a small city 80 miles away) for a long Easter weekend with her family, his first extended trip into a normal world. They were accompanied by one other child from the home and by another staff member, Yvonne. The trip was intended to help assess Gary's capacity to live in a home should one become available. Following is the staff report of Gary's first reaction to living for a brief time with a family.

From the moment we left the institution, Gary absorbed everything. He asked questions of my friend Yvonne (whom he'd never met before) all the way to the station. At the station, his eyes moved rapidly in curiosity from one thing to another. On the train, he sat quietly, observing the people passing in the aisles, and the trains, cars, and scenery passing by the window. He made frequent enquiries and comments. He appeared relaxed and confident. He became restless a couple of times during the trip and once asked to go for a walk through the car. At one point he sat for three or four minutes studying the people across the aisle, then called, "Man, I'm going to play in Liz's house." He and the man chatted for some time.

When it started to get dark, he was fascinated by the reflection in the window and asked at one point if everyone was asleep. He was quiet when we arrived at the station in Peterborough, and didn't want to get into my father's car. It was dark in the car and we assumed that was partly the reason for his hesitation. At the house he stood for about two minutes and took stock of the situation and then proceeded to investigate the house and cross-examine my family. He ate supper with three adults, my nine-year-old sister, and Yvonne. After supper he discovered upstairs a stuffed dog which he carried around periodically during the weekend. He went to bed willingly and settled quickly with Yvonne beside him.

Friday he spent all morning inspecting things. He carried several little items (e.g., a doll's bottle, a pepper grinder) around until he lost interest in them. He played for about half an hour in the basement with my young sister and her friend, interested in their rope-skipping. He later dragged the skipping rope upstairs and strung it all over the house. He seemed confused by the plan of the house and two or three times went into the linen cupboard instead of the bathroom. When my parents went to church, he seemed overly concerned about whether they would return. He stood at the door and called to them until they disappeared.

He thoroughly enjoyed lunch, as he did every meal with my family. With his amusing behaviour he was the centre of attraction, and frequently broke into a warm smile or spontaneous laughter in response to adult attention.

At rest time, he accepted being left alone with Patty to go to sleep, but he remained awake for almost an hour, whispering to himself and playing with the stuffed dog.

In the afternoon we all drove to a farm. He enjoyed the twenty-minute drive and kept asking repeatedly for us to sing. When we arrived at the farm house, he immediately began inspecting the items in all the rooms. He chatted with all the strangers and was curious about everything. At the barn he hesitated for a couple of minutes and then, clutching Yvonne's hand tightly, he ventured inside and showed enthusiasm for all the unusual sights. He shuddered once when a cow bellowed, but laughed when it occurred the second and third times. He heaved a sigh of relief upon returning outdoors.

Saturday he awakened at 5:30 a.m., crying because his hand was stuck down the side of the bed, but was quickly comforted by Yvonne. He spent Saturday morning puttering around the house with my sister, Dianne, and played for some time in the basement, pasting, cutting, and colouring with Dianne and Patty. He enjoyed helping my mother put the groceries away and insisted on being told what was in every can and package. He was delighted with the term, "yes siree," which my mother used and repeated it often the rest of the weekend to provoke laughter from everyone.

That day we went downtown. He was tense in the crowd (clung tightly to my hand) but didn't display his anxiety. He enjoyed browsing through a store that wasn't busy and purchased a pair of sun-glasses which he wore the rest of the weekend. This amused the adults. Gary thrived on this attention, but wasn't aggressive about attaining it.

He spent another busy morning Sunday with his sunglasses, the presents from the Easter Bunny, and played with water in the basement with Dianne. After lunch he refused to go upstairs for rest. Yvonne eventually had to carry him up, and after much ado he reluctantly accepted bed. He again lay awake for a long period, arguing with Patty about a couple of bracelets he had been sporting all morning. When I entered the room, he immediately hid them under the covers along with sun-glasses, saying they were gone and objecting strongly when I took them from him.

Later, during the two-hour drive back to the city, Gary spent his time slapping powder and lipstick from Yvonne's purse on his face, and singing spontaneously from time to time. When we left him with an unfamiliar adult in his unit at the institution, he was choking back big tears in a gallant attempt to be brave.

By April (fifteen months after the beginning of treatment) when he was three years and eleven months old, Gary's behaviour was hardly the same as it had been at the beginning of the rehabilitation programme. He was showing much more initiative in his nursery school play, both indoors and outdoors. His span of concentration seemed close to that of a normal child in nursery school, averaging ten to fifteen minutes with advanced toys. He was being imaginative, putting dolls to bed, spanking them, feeding them, feeding himself, and looking at himself in the mirror. He could co-operate well in play with another child, and seldom needed to refer to the teacher for help in using a toy or retrieving one from another child. When frustrated, he sulked much less frequently. Outside of nursery school he was showing a capacity to amuse himself: he looked at books, used crayons, and made imaginative use of creative materials.

Gary was finally taking responsibility in routines (eating, dressing, using the toilet, sleeping). He was completely toilet trained and could demonstrate his self-sufficiency by going to the toilet on his own. He enjoyed eating, although showing strong dislikes for a few foods. Bed-time had become a thoroughly pleasant situation between the staff and Gary. His earlier habit of rocking diminished.

With his greatly improved speech, Gary was able to reveal more of his inner world. He was making comments about materials and experiences and desperately trying to pick up information by asking questions. Although his sentence structure was poor and his language was not up to the level of his curiosity, he continued to communicate in an eager, rather anxious way. His general demeanour was appealing now, and the staff members were feeling highly rewarded by his responsiveness and enthusiasm. He seemed to have a warm relationship with many of the unit mothers.

Throughout the next five months, Gary continued to make steady progress, seemingly feeling more and more secure within himself. His relationships with children and adults continued to grow in depth; he became more venturesome in play; his speech showed marked improvement in clarity and sentence structure; and his adjustment to the routines of eating, sleeping, bathing and using the toilet remained a happy one.

In an attempt to expand his world and broaden his experiences, the staff placed him in a community nursery school when he was four years and four months of age. Here he made a satisfactory and happy adjustment to both the new school and the staff. He had sufficient self-confidence to go by himself in a taxi. He enjoyed having his own library card; going to the library with the staff, selecting his own books and taking them home to "read." Because of his enthusiasm for outside experiences, he was taken once more to Peterborough for a weekend visit. This time he seemed more relaxed and easy, and worked in as one of the family. He particularly enjoyed helping the father of the house, and at one time claimed, "He's *my* daddy too."

At four years and five months of age, Gary seemed ready for adoption placement. His trust in adults seemed steady and there were indications of self-trust as well. It appeared that he could now take a much larger world in his stride, given loving, sensitive parents who could meet his needs and be patient with his inadequacies. When a home was found and Gary was introduced to it and his prospective parents, he seemed like a young man in love. Happy and carefree, he would climb on anyone's knee to talk about it. Slow placement seemed the best plan for Gary, as it was for most of the children, so for a month there were almost daily visits between parents and child. Gradually, their time together was increased, from visits to the zoo, to walks in the vicinity of the institution, to days in his new home, then to the final stage of overnight and week-end visits. After a month, Gary was more than ready for placement, yearning to stay with his adoptive mother and father (whom he adored), and finally crying and uncomfortable when left at the institution by his prospective parents. On the day of placement, he greeted his mother with open arms and seemed totally aware that life at the institution was over for him. "I'm going to live with Mr. and Mrs. K. Patty went away to her mother and daddy and never came back. So did Billy. And now I'm going and won't be back to see you."

Gary was an example of a submissive, disinterested child whose slow response to treatment culminated in a startling unfolding of personality which disclosed a small child crying out for affection and satisfying experiences. When these were offered, he was able to develop a compatible relationship with adults which paved the way, later on, for feelings of trust and dependency.

11

Paddy

SECURITY SCORES

Age	Score (Pre-school Mental Health Assessment Form)
3 years 3 months	37
3 years 5 months	13
3 years 9 months	15
4 years	34
4 years 3 months	34
4 years 7 months	28
4 years 11 months	34

AN INCIDENT marked the end of an old life and the beginning of a new one for this four-year-old boy, reared in the institution since early infancy. One day, as the supervisor was chatting with two volunteers, an eager, sturdy, blue-eyed, blond boy came to the office door on his way home from the community nursery school.

"Who are those ladies, Miss K.?" he asked.

"Come on in and see them, Paddy," was the reply.

"Are they friends of boys and girls, like my Irene and George?" asked Paddy, as he strolled self-confidently into the room.

"What's your name?" he asked, turning to the woman, and then with a nod he said, "My name is Paddy O'Mallory, but it is *going to be* Paddy Brown."

Crawling affectionately to the supervisor's knee, he grasped her face between his hands, and looking intently into her eyes, said "Do you know what? Irene and George are going to be my mommy and daddy and I'm going to live with them, and won't see you ever again."

Then, with eyes aglow, and an air of self-confidence, he swaggered down the hall to his unit mother.

Paddy exemplified the kind of child who was able to make exceptionally good use of the rehabilitation programme. Once positive psychological development was started, he could be observed undergoing weekly improvements in behaviour. Basically a fearful youngster, he needed help in facing each new experience and in getting through it. Once it was assimilated, however, he seemed to emerge a stronger, steadier child, standing ready to benefit from the next experience which would lead him on to further maturity and self-confidence. He was finally capable of putting down roots in a family, and of approaching life with a lively assertiveness that was both rewarding and delightful to see.

Phase I of Treatment

When first observed in this institution, Paddy was three years and three months of age. He was generally timid and passive, and sucked him thumb constantly. The staff acquired little knowledge of his personality for the first few months, and it was not until he was three years and five months of age that we began to have a reliable record of his behaviour. His security score was very low (13) and remained substantially the same for the next four months (15 at three years, nine months of age).

He seemed to be avoiding contact with other children, frequently withdrawing from their play, seemingly preferring to play by himself. He was usually timid and submissive toward the other children, but occasionally could show resistance to them and at times would tease.

When the treatment programme started, Paddy was showing such compulsive characteristics as insisting that all doors be closed and chronically sucking his thumb. He was tearful at the sight of a car and would scream if taken for a ride in one. He felt overwhelmed by each new situation he faced, and would avoid venturesome play requiring any physical effort. He was so lacking in trust in adults that any physical or emotional upset could not be reduced by proffered comfort. He would scream, run away, cry excessively, and struggle violently to get away from a sympathetic adult. Ten minutes would sometimes elapse before his sobbing would subside and he would settle emotionally. Such behaviour worked against his successful rehabilitation, as it required considerable forbearance on the part of an adult to deal with him kindly.

His play with materials and equipment was immature. Both his indoor play and outdoor play were aimless, and he seemed incapable of settling down to any constructive activity unless closely supervised and encouraged by an adult. If he wished to play with a toy already being used by another child, any diverting by the teacher precipitated a temper tantrum or prolonged crying. At times he was quite indifferent to the toys, while at other times, when interested, he was irritable if he could not make the toy work.

As the first few months elapsed, he showed some increase in the capacity to amuse himself with the toys, occasionally showing interest for about half an hour. For several months, he had a compulsion to carry balls with him wherever he went.

His response to the staff was fraught with conflict and lack of trust. While able to respond to demonstrations of affection, he frequently refused any direction given him, responding by having temper tantrums. At other times he accepted direction and enjoyed being cared for and helped. He even occasionally sought physical comfort from familiar staff members, while rebuffing it at other times. Screaming temper tantrums were frequently encountered; he was fearful and apprehensive with unfamiliar adults. He responded to encouragement to help himself in dressing, both when getting up in the morning and when getting into outdoor clothing. Although slow, he was co-operative, and relied on the staff for assistance.

He responded rapidly to toilet training after a preliminary period of anxiety, expressed through constant demands to go to the toilet, and by whining, crying, and becoming generally upset. Within a short while, he was completely trained.

Like many of the children in the institution, Paddy found eating one of his real satisfactions, and for this reason few problems appeared in the dining room, even after a change in food and eating habits was initiated. Paddy ate most foods with enthusiasm, co-operatively carrying out the meal-time procedure and feeding himself skilfully. In this situation, he was able to take direction from and be controlled even by a strange member of staff.

Bedtime was relatively easy for Paddy. His chronic thumb-sucking was most marked at this time of day and seemed to give him great comfort. He was able to accept the bed-time routine, and to relax and sleep soundly both at daily rest time and at night. He could easily accept a change in procedure or a strange staff member and would always wake up cheerful.

By September, 1958, Paddy's world had expanded somewhat. In June, he had been sent to a community morning nursery group as a companion to another child who was also going. This experiment had not been successful, since he stood by the door, refused to go inside, and watched passively, sucking hard on his thumb. After three mornings of this behaviour, the staff decided he was not yet ready to take on this new experience and he was withdrawn from the community nursery school. In its place he was given enriched play experiences and the opportunity to develop warm relationships with adults by going to the newly opened nursery school in the garden coach house of the institution. In addition, he acquired a volunteer mother who broadened his world with rides on street cars, walks in parks, jaunts through department stores, and finally visits to her home, including the opportunity to stay for supper and participate in the family life.

Phase II of Treatment

Gradually, Paddy began to show signs of enjoying the world around him and less and less time was spent gazing solemnly around with his thumb in his mouth. Although at first going out with his volunteer mother was fraught with fear and apprehension, he gradually was able to look forward to the experiences she had to offer. By September, although still preferring one familiar adult, he was able to co-operate often with other people's requests and accept the enforcement of rules by several members of the staff. He began first of all to accept demonstrations of affection by the staff and eventually would ask for them. He still showed undue emotion if hurt and cried about ten minutes despite whatever reassurances an adult would give him. There seemed to be real improvement in his relationships with the other children. He was beginning to enjoy a limited amount of social activity, playing well for short periods of time and then withdrawing to play quietly by himself. His whole attitude to life was becoming more venturesome, and his willingness to cope with new experiences thrust upon him by a changing world was reflected in his play outdoors and indoors. His attention span was still very short and highly dependent upon close supervision by an adult. He was generally co-operative and happy in the routines of eating, sleeping, washing, and using the toilet, although he still needed considerable adult prompting to remind him to make a consistent effort. His speech was now clear, although still limited to phrases. In October, a move to a smaller unit with five other children and an understanding unit mother seemed to contribute greatly to Paddy's well-being. He began to trust, to speak more, and to enjoy the other children. His contact with and interest in his volunteer mother's television set may have contributed somewhat to his spurt in speech development. After nine months, Paddy seemed to be developing some feelings of dependency and trust, showed some curiosity about a widening world, and was willing to initiate some effort on his own.

A year after the treatment programme had begun, an attempt was made to give him a mental test. Prior to this time, Paddy, like many of the other children, would have shown severe retardation on testing, because of a lack of developmental experiences. Even at this time, the tester found it most difficult to establish a working relationship with him. An even later test, fifteen months after treament had begun, showed some of the same disturbing symptoms, although Paddy was generally more normal, showing greater emotional expression and establishing a more realistic relationship with the tester. The second test reflected the effect of treatment by a much more diversified response to the variety of tasks presented. Paddy seemed to be functioning within the Dull Normal range, although this could not be regarded as a definitive rating.

By December (a year after the treatment programme had begun), there was a heartening increase in Paddy's security score, which was maintained over the next ten months. The increase seemed to be a reflection of the comfort which he felt in the protection offered by a small unit with a trustworthy house mother, and which he demonstrated in most of the situations within the institution. His feeling of security was apparent in his improved relationships with the other children, in his greater ability to use play materials constructively, in his acceptance of more of the staff members, and in a satisfactory attitude toward routines. He was talking clearly in sentences. He still found difficulty in unfamiliar situations, which remained a source of apprehension and precipitated negative behaviour. For example, when leaving the building for a new trip, Paddy had to be carried out of the door screaming. He still showed a deep-seated fear of animals.

Phase III of Treatment

Fifteen months of treatment seemed to bring about a sufficiently marked recovery in Paddy that it could be regarded as permanent. He now seemed on the threshold of a new world, standing ready to step into a wider community which would offer more challenge to him. His step-by-step gain in self-confidence and his desire to do increasingly more for himself had been fascinating to watch. It had always been necessary to push him into new experiences either in the nursery school or in the world outside the institution. He always needed very strong support from dependable adults in each new experience, and many times he had to be physically carried through situations which he resisted with screams and tears. Each time, he

seemed to gain in stature and come through ready to move on to the
next challenge. Each time he seemed to show conflict between his
fear of the new and his feelings of boredom or dislike for the old
routine.

At this time, Paddy was transferred to a family unit where he was
the oldest child of the group of five. He now had the capacity to
handle this new social situation very well. His affectionate, sympathetic, and sociable qualities which had been emerging were given scope
in the opportunity to be "paternal" towards the other children. He
loved to help dress them, cuddle them, and lead them by the hand
to the dining room. He would visit the house mother of his last unit
for companionable chats. He would visit younger children and solici-
tously discuss things with them. He was observed sitting on a younger
child's bed, with the child's head on his knees, patting her and at the
same time sucking his thumb. One day when he was in bed with a
cold, two of the other children climbed up on his bed in order that
Paddy might show them a picture book. He would sometimes instigate
games with the other children of his unit, romping and playing for a
short time.

Paddy now seemed to be seeking dependable adults who would
support him in each fresh approach to his exciting new world. He was
interested in people and curious about their living arrangements:
"What's your name?" "Where's your home?" "Have you got a sister?"
"Where is your bed?" At this stage in Paddy's treatment, a broader
environment was sought to test his apparent security. One of the staff
members took him to her home in a small city eighty miles from
Toronto. He was accompanied by Gary. The reaction to this new
experience was recorded in detail. At first, he was apprehensive but
curious about the people in the station and in the moving train.
Gradually, he was able to enjoy the train, becoming apprehensive
again only when meeting Miss M's family at the station and riding
home in the car with them. He refused to join the family for lunch,
but sat close to Miss M. in another room where they ate alone. In the
evening, he seemed to need the security of the staff member to sleep
with him.

The next morning was spent exploring the house, watching the
activities of the father, playing for a short while with a younger sister,
and returning to Miss M. frequently for reassurance that she was still
there. In the afternoon, everyone went to a farm. In the words of
Miss M., "Paddy was very anxious, refusing to go into the barn to
see the animals, although he insisted on being held a safe distance

from the door. He was interested in the horse that he could see standing just inside. He asked repeatedly, even after we were well on our
way back to the car, if the animals were tied and if they slept in the
barn all by themselves. He sang all the way to and from the farm in
the car, and, on his return home related all his experiences to my
mother, telling her 'Paddy was afraid.' He seemed surprisingly at ease
at supper with the entire family.

"After supper, my sister's fiancé was 'rough-housing' with me. This
alarmed Paddy, and he withdrew from John. He asked several times
if John had hurt me, and even after going upstairs to bed, insisted
that John was a bad boy. Once more he insisted that I lie beside him
but he went to sleep quickly and slept quietly. The next day he
refused to go downstairs and finally had to be carried. He looked
quickly to the chair where John had been sitting, seemed to relax and
wanted to be put down.

"The rest of the morning passed happily and uneventfully. In the
afternoon, Paddy was taken down town shopping, where he became
tense and nervous in the crowd. He rocked, sucked his thumb, and
asked to be held. We phoned my Dad to rescue us and Paddy talked
on the telephone, saying 'Paddy wants you to take him home. Don't
like down town.'"

That evening he was much more venturesome with the family, inter-
acting with them and needing little reassurance from Miss M. He had
even the courage to sulk when not permitted to dry the dishes, and
at bed time slept readily with Gary. The next day he seemed completely easy with the family, seeking them out and asking questions.
There was an occasional flash of jealousy when Gary was around and
he needed considerable assurance that he was liked just as much as
the other boy. On the whole, Paddy was happy and relaxed over the
long weekend, but there would be times when he would suddenly
lapse into thumb-sucking and remain quiet from three to ten minutes.
At one point he registered astonishment when Miss M. was kissed by
her father. He sat looking wistful for some time and then said, "Do
you like your daddy?" "Did he kiss you?"

Adoption Placement

It was judged in March, 1959, that Paddy was now ready to adapt
to and make use of an adoptive or foster placement which could provide him with love and with dependable, understanding parents. He,
in turn, could be rewarding to a foster parent with his qualities of
sociability and enthusiasm for living. By April, potential adoptive

parents had been found who were eager for a little boy and were willing to co-operate with the institution staff by going through a long pre-placement period. A series of visits by the prospective parents to Paddy at the institution, jaunts to places in the community, trips with Paddy to their home, and week-end sojourns, finally culminated in adoptive placement by the end of June, nineteen months after treatment had begun.

During this pre-placement period, Paddy noticeably grew away from his unit mother toward a new dependency on his adoptive mother. A few weeks before placement he was heard to say to his unit mother, who was preoccupied with some of the other children, "You're busy, Lisa, I'll go down to supper by myself."

Pre-placement Visits

The story of Paddy's placement demonstrates how, ideally, the institution staff was able to make use of community services, prospective parents, and the facilities of the institution. It was decided that Paddy must meet his prospective adoptive parents casually in a park, and there make contact with them as he played about with his unit mother. The next step was to have the adoptive parents take him for short walks in the vicinity of the institution, gradually extending them further for visits to stores and churches, etc. Finally, Paddy was taken to their home for a visit, pyjamas were bought for him, and his own bed pointed out for him. Although talking freely about his pyjamas and bed, he refused to stay overnight for many weeks. A baseball hat, purchased by his adoptive parents, was more successful and was securely clapped to his head for afternoon naps.

As soon as a firm relationship was established with his adoptive mother, Paddy was sent to a community nursery school rather than to the one in the institution, in an attempt to broaden his experiences and increase his capacity to deal with a greater variety of people. The job of taking him on the first day was delegated to his adoptive mother. For the first day he clung to her skirts, refusing to move away; the second morning he stood all the time and watched the other children; the third morning he was able to join the activity in a cautious way.

More and more as Paddy moved toward adoption placement, a maturity appeared in the routines of his life. He took greater responsibility for his own cleanliness, adhered more to regulations in the dining room, and, although showing preference for familiar staff members, was co-operative and comfortable with all. Nevertheless, there were still intense symptoms of insecurity, particularly when Paddy was faced with a new situation, such as a picnic. When told he was going to be taken, he balked, saying that he had never been to a picnic. Because the staff thought he was ready to benefit from this new experience, he was carried out the door to the waiting taxi, screaming and kicking. Once at the picnic, he cheered up, participated in all activities enthusiastically and came home proudly telling everyone in the building about his new experience. He still over-reacted to upsetting physical experiences, such as having his 'polio' needle. He had to be dragged bodily and held while the needle was put into his arm. For the rest of the day, whenever he caught sight of his arm, he would whimper and cry. His sensitivity to being corrected remained almost as intense as formerly. One night, after his house mother had sent him back to his room for disturbing others while watching television, he sat on the floor sucking his thumb, refusing either to play with his toys or to go to supper. Later he lay on his bed, still sucking his thumb, and when his house mother attempted to divert his attention and elicit his interest in something, he merely responded by "You go away," or, "I don't like you."

Casual notes taken by the staff indicated an improvement in Paddy's posture. Whereas he had formerly shown what we termed a typical institution "droop" with his total muscle tone lax, his mouth sagging open, and his lips protruding, from March onward there seemed to be a weekly gain. His posture seemed to straighten, his shoulders to broaden; his general muscle tone seemed firmer, and he walked with a springing gait which appeared to reflect increased self-confidence.

Paddy's placement into his adoptive home came in July and, like most of the placements, went through a delightful, "honeymoon" period, where the child aimed only to please. Everything was new and exciting, and conformity to the activities of the family provided the thrill of approval and acceptance. His adoptive family surrounded him with the protectiveness of homey experiences, giving praise and affection and showing sensitivity to his fears of any new things. It was still necessary to discuss with Paddy well ahead of time any new event he had to meet. His marked sociability led him quickly outdoors, seeking children to play with. He was able to play contentedly with them, feeling secure that his family was nearby.

First Stage of Adoption

Three months after adoptive placement, Paddy showed signs of having "put down roots." A very warm relationship had developed with his parents and he seemed to want to share his joy for living with them. He regarded everything as belonging to his mother, his father, and himself. He asked for and showed affection. Whenever he behaved unreasonably, he would afterward seek out extra demonstrations of affection. He was still very sensitive to criticism or discipline. On the whole, he was highly co-operative with his family.

He was eager to learn about everything. Every household routine seemed thrilling. He was generally rather cautious and obedient and no longer had long temper tantrums or behaved unsociably, as he had a year ago in the institution. His general facial expression was more relaxed, and he seemed to have lost his chronic anxiety. He was kindly toward other children and would withdraw from any quarrelling or bullying to return home and tell his mother about it. He was proud of his achievements and thrived on approval. His thumb-sucking was diminishing. He enjoyed his morning kindergarten, looked forward to it each day, and "bubbled" with enthusiastic stories on his return.

His social interest and his agility helped him to win friends easily. Although not aggressive with other children, he protected his own interests. He loved to participate in all activities, imitating the behaviour of others and showing imagination. However, he was still a highly distractible youngster who might benefit by more intellectual stimulation. He never stopped talking, asking questions relating past and present experiences, and trying to relate them in turn to the future. He delighted in showing slides of himself, his family, and his friends at the family's summer cottage. He enjoyed pointing out his relatives in these pictures, dwelling possessively on his relationship to them. He continued to take responsibility in dressing, eating, and using the toilet, and he took pride in his capacity to be independent.

Over his three-month period of adjustment to adoption placement, he vividly demonstrated a positive growth in self-confidence and developed an intense desire to belong to his family. He particularly delighted in imitating his father's actions. He had lost his apprehensiveness to such an extent that he could cope with experiences frightening to some children raised in normal home situations. For example, at the Santa Claus parade in Toronto, replete with fairy-tale figures, enormous floats, bands, and towering clowns, his enthusiasm knew no bounds. His eager face, peering out from hundreds of people gathered to watch, caught the attention of many of the passing clowns, who stopped to shake hands with him. A woman standing beside his mother commented: "I have been to this parade for years and years, but never have I enjoyed myself as much as this year, seeing it through the eyes of your little boy."

In January, six months after placement, Paddy seemed to be consolidating his status in his new home. He was now much more assertive and occasionally was difficult to manage. He had the courage to test the limits of some of the family rules and sometimes wore an expression that asked, "What are you going to do about it?" He was much less obedient than formerly. He required more mature reasons for following directions. Instead of always coming when called, he would now appear too busy to pay attention. His enthusiasm for life continued and frequently led to his becoming over-stimulated and out of bounds in his behaviour. He cried more spontaneously, but many of his fears were reduced, as he no longer seemed fearful of the dark, nor did he become anxious when faced with a new situation.

Although chatty and friendly with adults, he discriminated more carefully in the showing of particular favour. His relationship with other children continued to show healthy progress. He was a favourite with them. He liked to "boss" the younger ones, but was eager to learn from the older ones. He continued to be responsible in routines of eating, dressing, and sleeping. He was much more relaxed and now sucked his thumb less. His ability to concentrate with play materials was greater, and his play showed imagination. He brought home quite adequate art work for his age from school, and glowed with delight when praised by his parents.

Like many formerly institutionalized children, Paddy showed tremendous unevenness in his developmental pattern. He was up to his chronological level of maturity in some aspects of living, and well behind in others. That is, he was advanced in his social, in contrast to emotional, development. As he lived in his home, the wide difference in these aspects of development seemed to diminish concurrently with an apparent improvement in his feeling of well-being.

At the time of this writing, the future looks bright for Paddy. He is one of the children of whom we are confident to predict that emotional damage has not been permanent. We anticipate that he will continue through life with enthusiasm, adapting to the demands of his community and becoming a productive citizen. It seems safe to predict that his present capacity to understand and communicate with his adoptive parents and his contemporaries will continue to develop to include all those people who will be important to him.

12

Mindy

Age	Score (Pre-school Mental Health Assessment Form)
2 years 4 months	10
2 years 7 months	32
3 years	11
3 years 2 months	25
3 years 4 months	37
4 years	36
4 years 2 months	34

MINDY was of partly Oriental background. No birth records were available. She was admitted to the institution at four months of age with a functional heart murmur, which proved not to be serious, health records for the next two years showing merely a series of upper respiratory infections.

No psychological records were kept until she was two years, four months of age. At this time her security score was very low (ten). However, she responded quickly to treatment, and within a year her score had risen to 37. She was a sensitive, fearful child, very responsive to her adult world and rather charming in her manner toward grownups. When an opportunity for foster placement arose at this time, it was decided that Mindy had developed sufficient strength of personality to be ready for it.

The foster placement was one which would arouse apprehension under ordinary circumstances, as the Bell family already had four children and was expecting a fifth. A further hazard lay in the fact that one of the foster parents' children was the same age as Mindy. The house was small, but the atmosphere was warm and lively. The foster mother was particularly bright and interested in Mindy's problem. She regarded her as a challenge. The other children in the family were lively, alert, well-controlled, and self-directed; probably all more intelligent than Mindy. Most important, the family was willing to accept Mindy's racial background.

Since no other home was readily available, Mindy was placed with the Bells when she was three years and eight months of age. Twelve preliminary visits culminated in a successful weekend stay, followed by permanent placement, by which time, Mindy seemed ready for her new experiences.

After placement, Miss Kilgour and the foster mother worked together on a long-term plan to guide Mindy's adjustment to her new life and to help reduce some of the more serious difficulties which might arise in this rather tenuous situation. By means of close guidance, it was hoped that Mindy's foster placement might prepare her for successful life in a permanent home.

Mindy had been at the institution for two years when the new programme was inaugurated. This black-haired, olive-complexioned girl had appeared, after two months' treatment, to be a child whose whole world was undermined by fear and who failed to perceive people as human beings. She preferred to be by herself, away from other children, who were a source of disturbance to her. With them, she was aggressive and cross, fighting, hitting out, irritable, and insistent on her own way. She seemed fearful of physical experiences, avoiding adventuresome play and, when hurt, showing extreme emotion by screaming and crying. Although she sought adult reassurance when hurt, she refused to be comforted and would continue to scream. She habitually sucked her thumb during sleep, in routines, while playing, and when tired or upset.

Her play was sadly deficient, as she could not settle down to constructive effort either outdoors or indoors. She needed constant attention and adult guidance to keep her attending to a toy for even a short while. When unable to have a toy she particularly desired, or when expected to obey some of the rules of the playground or playroom, she would have temper tantrums, scream, cry, and protest. If a toy presented any difficulty to her, her tolerance to the resulting frustration was extremely limited and she would become impatient, irritable, and finally begin to scream.

There was considerable conflict in her attitudes toward adults. She responded to and even sought out physical affection and comfort, but on the other hand seemed fearful of help when it was offered and would refuse it by becoming highly emotional. She became upset in crowds and yet seemed to like adult company in a rather indiscriminate way. She showed resistance to the dressing routine by whining, pulling away, crying, showing impatience, and sometimes resorting to temper tantrums when she was directed through the procedure. If no one supervised or insisted on her dressing, she would remain inattentive and unconcerned about completing it.

Mindy accepted the toilet training routine in a matter-of-fact way but had little control. Eating was one of her main satisfactions; she enjoyed her food and meal-time routine and seemed to feel most satisfaction at these times. Her desire for food seemed greater than her apprehensions and she was able to accept new foods without protest and would tolerate strange adults in charge of the dining room. She seemed anxious that she might not be served her food and would become restless and scream while waiting her turn. Contrary to the relative easiness shown in the routines of dining and using the toilet, sleep time was a disturbed and disturbing one for her. When a staff member was in the room settling the children, Mindy could accept the procedure without too much protest. However, once left without the help of an adult, she would regularly get out of bed, protest, whine, and cry. If she remained in bed, she would have temper tantrums, scream, and, standing in her crib, would rock back and forth from one foot to another. She slept poorly, rolling about, seemingly disturbed. She constantly sucked her thumb.

After a year of progressive treatment which included nursery school experience (eventually daily), a volunteer mother, a warm attachment to a house mother, and the opportunity to live regularly with a small group of children, Mindy's behaviour showed marked changes, and she seemed much more secure. Although she was still basically fearful, almost every aspect of the life she was leading now seemed easier and more normal. Her relationship with the other children in the institution was greatly improved.

She showed irritability at times by striking out and biting, but she generally enjoyed the presence of the others and got along well with them during play time. She could hold her own and insist on her own rights, but she would also share and accept the fact that the other children must take turns and have toys. She did not mind sharing the attention of even her favourite adult with the other children.

Her ability to concentrate on play materials had improved tremendously. She was enjoying strenuous physical activity with the outdoor equipment and showed an interest in playing with a wide variety of indoor playthings. She played best when alone, particularly enjoying imaginative play. She tended still to wait a long time before asking for help from an adult when in difficulty with toys, an attitude which suggested that dependent trust was still underdeveloped. She was still terrified of animals and panicky at the sight of blood. But whereas she had formerly screamed with terror at new experiences, such as the sight of a butterfly or the sensation of a breeze on her face, she now could enjoy trips on streetcars and visits to stores. She was curious about unusual things, such as clowns, and enjoyed seeing Santa Claus as part of the Christmas festivities. She was still a chronic thumb sucker, and frequently would masturbate prior to falling asleep.

Mindy now seemed to have developed some degree of dependence, albeit tenuous, on the adults she knew best. She was generally ready to accept help and direction regarding routines, and would eventually seek out comfort from adults and be reassured by it. On some occasions she felt assured enough of her status to argue with an adult who might criticize or correct her. Although generally co-operative and interested in dressing and undressing herself, she would refuse to wear clothes which she had torn or got dirty and occasionally she would insist on choosing the clothes she was to wear. If this privilege was refused, she would sulk. Eating continued to be an enjoyable diversion, with Mindy co-operative and ready to take responsibility whenever possible. She was beginning to express definite dislikes, and with her new enjoyment of the other children she was sometimes over-talkative at the table. By now she was completely toilet trained. In several areas of her life she was taking responsibility for looking after herself. Sleep time had become a rather normal and pleasant episode of the day. She depended on adult help to settle down in bed and, after some preliminary quiet play, could relax and sleep soundly. She could accept unfamiliar sleeping arrangements with equanimity and usually woke up in a cheerful frame of mind.

Pre-placement Planning

On the basis of her improvement, Mindy was selected for a foster home placement in a family which could accept her mixed racial background. Although the Bell family already numbered four, it was uniquely thoughtful and warm toward its new member. The mother was prepared to work with Mindy to help her over her most difficult times of adjustment. The older foster children were surprisingly sensitive to her problems. We anticipated that Mindy would display highly controlled behaviour which would mask her feelings when first placed. Therefore, considerable pre-placement work had been done before launching her into a new world of family living. Instead of being kept at the institution nursery school, she was enrolled in a community nursery school where she was instantly introduced to a programme geared to the needs of normal children. Here she attempted to keep up with the other children and to maintain social relationships with them. So intense was her effort that she seemed to become exhausted both emotionally and physically, so her attendance was reduced to three days weekly. Mindy's introduction to her foster family was made very slowly, with her familiar and trusted volunteer mother participating in the visits.

Twelve visits were made in all, the whole foster family first coming to the institution for a chat with Mindy on home ground. After this, Mindy was taken to the foster home by both the institution's social worker and the volunteer mother. Mindy accepted the trip with outward composure and little display of anxiety. However, during one visit when the foster family was popping corn, her composure crumbled. Mindy leapt into the worker's arms and needed considerable reassurance before she could finally bring herself to cautiously approach the popcorn. Gradually, the visits were lengthened and Mindy became familiar with the home routine and the children, developing a "pal" relationship with the child who was her contemporary. Little by little Mindy showed a desire to return to the foster home and to leave the institution behind. On her first overnight visit, she displayed no anxiety about sleeping in a strange bed, and by the time she was able to stay a weekend, she seemed ready to move into her new world.

Her response to placement was characterized by conformity, a lack of feeling, and a peculiar "blanking out" when under stress. She immediately took an intense liking to her foster father and had a look for him alone. (This was surprising in view of a former longstanding fear of men.) Now she generally preferred men to women, and tended to make overtures of friendships to them indiscriminately. She accepted her foster mother as a source of authority and anxiously did everything requested or expected of her in an attempt to ingratiate herself. So fearful was she of criticism that, for a period of time, she would cease all activity and sit frozen if the foster mother entered the room or peeked in to see what she was doing. After the first three or four months, although she expressed no direct hostility, she developed enough courage to give her mother fierce looks when she was corrected. Her refusal to conform took the form of "pulling a blank look" and acting as if she had not heard. The pattern of total withdrawal also appeared when Mindy was put under any stress. It therefore did not become a matter of concern until a few months after placement, when it was thought that she was ready for less permissiveness and more insistence on conformity to the family routines. When attempts were made to have her learn simple prayers and remember family rules, or when she was in a crowd, she would appear confused, would not ask for help, and would mask any emotion by an expressionless face. She seemed particularly unnerved by any excitement or change of routine. She was most comfortable and functioned best when her life was highly controlled and organized and she could anticipate what was to come next.

The children in the Bell home, contrary to our fears, played a salutary role in Mindy's adjustment. They welcomed her enthusiastically and she accepted them and enjoyed their company. She was able to act out a "baby" role with the oldest sister who was particularly tactful with her. In the past months she had come to regard the child of the same age as herself as her constant playmate. It was only later that she regarded him as a threat. The two-year-old in the family was particularly bright and alert to her environment and was, in many ways, as advanced as Mindy in living experiences. Therefore Mindy could play with her as a contemporary, feeling no inadequacy in her capacity to keep up.

One of the disturbing aspects of Mindy's personality on first placement was her apparent lack of feeling toward the other people with whom she lived. Although she would respond appropriately to affection, there seemed to be little true warmth in her gestures. One incident when Mindy tipped over the baby's carriage causing a messy and rather frightening nose-bleed concerned the foster mother. Instead of showing any concern, guilt, or sympathy, Mindy stood by ignoring the screams and the mess and was unmoved when the mother came to the rescue. Many months were to elapse before Mindy could shows signs of any sympathy for others. Only after a year did her foster mother feel that Mindy had any real affection for her. Only then, too, did Mindy show any capacity to shed tears over her own disappointments.

One of the positive qualities of Mindy's personality which carried over into her foster placement was her capacity to concentrate well on play materials. Although showing little animation or initiative and no creativity in play, she would imitate and follow the activity of the other children with real interest. The routine aspects of Mindy's life continued to progress without trouble. She slept well, used the toilet on her own, and was co-operative and interested in dressing. Mealtimes continued to be enjoyable. Only after ten or twelve months did she have the courage to express a definite dislike for particular foods or to show any resistance to going to bed at night. But even this was mild.

One Year after Placement

A year after foster home placement, Mindy still appeared over-conforming, meticulous, and capable only of rather shallow feelings; but occasional flashes of decisive behaviour seemed to indicate that some depth might be acquired in her relationships with other people. Although apparently indifferent to correction at the time it was given, she was very conforming and anxious when a similar situation arose again. While making friendly advances indiscriminately to all strangers, she sought out her foster father particularly for displays of physical affection. Still mainly anxious and conforming with adults, particularly her foster mother, she was beginning to show resistance to the children and could fight back occasionally in an open display of hostility. She showed a desire to compete with the foster child who was her contemporary but frequently resorted to sneaky, underhand methods. She could tell tall tales, point out the other child's misdemeanours, and sneak food from the cupboard, denying she had it; she even encouraged the two-year-old to break the family rules in an attempt to precipitate trouble.

Her need for praise, approval, and affection was much greater than that of the other children so she tended to be over-talkative and charming with adults. Unfortunately, she tended to talk *at* people rather than *with* them. She remained superficially cheerful most of the time, with a rare relaxation into a spell of sulking. She was almost totally devoid of spontaneous humor, seldom smiling, but responding with a smile to one from an adult. She could not join in the family jokes or teasing, but did enjoy silly and boisterous behaviour in the other children, although she did not participate herself. Jokes and fun seemed only to confuse her. One night at bedtime the foster mother chased the children squealing upstairs for sleep. They all piled under the bed, laughing uproariously, with the foster mother calling jokingly for them to come out. Whereas the rest of the children laughed even harder, Mindy immediately crawled out, and with a very intense expression said quickly, "Here I am Mommy." She seemed thoroughly confused when the fun continued for a short while.

She was anxious to obey all the family rules, even minor ones, and any indication of discipline set up strong concern in her. She wanted to take on chores for approval. Whereas formerly she could not ask for help and comfort when hurt or in difficulties, now she would occasionally do so, although the adult usually had to go to her with an offer of assistance or comfort. She could now admit there were some things she could not do. Although still showing little overt emotion, she now could cry more readily than before.

Her behaviour was still almost totally imitative. She never initiated activities. She tended to be destructive with the other children's possessions, apparently for the sake of the attention she created by it. On the other hand, she enjoyed and was enjoyed by the other children who were delighted to accept her as their sister. Mindy's compliant behaviour was very acceptable in routines, and as a result no real difficulties were encountered over dressing, eating, sleeping, or use of the toilet. Some advance had been made towards a less compulsive attitude towards food. No longer did Mindy gobble everything voraciously; she could now refuse what she did not like.

Prognosis

Looking back, one could see decided progress in Mindy's mental health and in her capacity to adjust to normal living. Looking ahead, it would appear that much of the success of Mindy's life will continue to be related to the astute controls imposed by this understanding foster family who are now willing to keep her permanently. It will be necessary for Mindy to have a clearly defined and well-articulated set of rules by which she can live. Without these she will have little in herself to give her behaviour direction and control. She will probably continue to require far more demonstrations of affection and words of encouragement than the other children in the family. Despite the fact that her intellectual status has risen from dull normal to average within the year, she will probably not do as well as the other children in school. The other children have the ability to tackle new problems; Mindy has not. She will be hampered also by her lack of capacity to concentrate on an unfamiliar task. Her anxiety for acceptance will probably always leave her vulnerable to even minor approval from both good and harmful influences in the community. She will be easily led into whatever is the current popular course of action, not only by her foster family, but by whatever group she might happen to join. She will undoubtedly be attracted to a person who can control her with a strong hand.

13

Louise

SECURITY SCORES

Age	Score*
18 months	+0.16
21 months	+0.19
2 years 1 month	8
2 years 2 months	29
2 years 10 months	9
3 years 1 month	21
3 years 4 months	26

*Scores for ages under two years are from the Infant Security Scale. All other scores are from the Pre-school Mental Health Assessment Form.

LOUISE was placed in an adoptive home only thirteen months after the treatment programme had begun, and before much individual attention could be given each child. The placement was made to the home of her volunteer mother who became enamoured of her charm and struck by her apparent need of special people. Because the family had no other children, and Louise seemed to attach herself to them with considerable intensity, there seemed no reason to discourage placement.

However, the staff was apprehensive, fearing that Louise, although an attractive, charming child, was not yet ready for life in a home with two eager parents. Her relationship with the volunteer mother had been of only three months' duration, and it was felt that her childless volunteer family were being swept away by the emotional appeal of a child needing a home. Attempts on the part of the staff to delay the adoption plans until Louise had reaped more benefit from individual treatment within the institution met with overwhelming emotional and political pressure from the prospective parents, resulting in early placement for Louise. Unfortunately, supervision of the child in her home was to be carried out by an adoption worker who knew little about Louise and her problems. Those people in the institution who knew her best could not carry out the adoption placement because of administrative procedures, and so their contact with Louise and her family was broken. To add some safeguard to the placement, the period of adoption probation (a waiting time before final legal custody is taken by the parents) was set at a year, rather than the usual six months.

Louise had been a blonde, blue-eyed, sturdily built baby when she was placed in the institution at six months of age. Prior to this time, time, her mother had tried to keep her on a welfare allowance, and had placed her with any woman who was willing to take care of her. When first placed in the institution, Louise had cried so much that she was put on phenobarbitol for a period of time. For the next year, brief medical records gave us the only information we had about Louise. She was treated for swollen glands and sore throat, rashes, impetigo, a boil, and chicken pox. Exactly a year after coming to the institution, she was again put on phenobarbitol.

At this time, her first mental health report gave us some insight into her psychological state. Like most of the children, Louise was finding satisfaction in food, and as a result few difficulties were encountered in her eating habits. She took to spoon-feeding, loved both her bottle and solids, accepted new foods without protesting, and would co-operate with anyone who would feed her. So eager was she for food that she resented any delay.

She was a restless sleeper, crying out and pitching about in her bed. She insisted always on lying in the same position to go to sleep. She was generally co-operative about toilet training, although no success had been achieved by the time she was eighteen months of age. She enjoyed her bath and showed no particular preference for any adult who bathed her. She merely tolerated any adult attempt to play with her energetically. She enjoyed being cuddled, but was easily upset and would sulk or cry for a long time when her feelings were hurt.

Unlike most of the children, she rather enjoyed environmental changes, if they were not too extreme. She liked to ride in her carriage. Her physical activity had been limited to bouncing in her cot or rocking back and forth on her feet. Being picked up to be dressed, washed, or fed provided a welcome relief from this boredom. She rarely vocalized (spoke or cried) even when stimulated. Her behaviour showed a compulsive character by her insistence on being clean and tidy.

She was generally indifferent towards people, and listless in their presence. However, there was a certain moodiness in her behaviour which showed itself in occasional flashes of jealousy when other children received adult attention. At times she would assert herself with other children by hanging on to toys and becoming upset if they were taken away. On occasion she even appeared shy and withdrawing rather than merely indifferent. Although her attention span was disappointingly short and she tended to flit from one thing to another, she was showing an interest in playthings, picking them up eagerly, but rapidly exhausting their possibilities. Mental testing indicated low average development.

At twenty-one months of age, after three months of the treatment programme, assessments indicated little essential change in Louise's mental health. There was some improvement in her ability to relax in bed, as she was no longer restless and now slept soundly, but she had begun to protest when first put to bed. Now she occasionally cried when placed on the toilet. Whereas formerly she had tolerated boisterous play in an indifferent way, she now registered fear and would cry when an adult attempted to play with her energetically.

She was extremely active and restless and continued to rock from one foot to the other for long periods of time. At times she was happy in a restricted play area (a nursery ward), and at other times, though rarely, she would cry and whine miserably when alone. She was no longer compulsive about cleanliness, and seemed unconcerned whether she was messy or dirty.

Her relationships with people seemed to reflect conflict. Although she was generally indifferent and apathetic towards others, there were times when she seemed very much aware of their presence. She wanted social contacts but would initially back away from both adults or children, only slowly relaxing over a period of days in the presence of new people.

Her play with toys was even more erratic than formerly. She permitted the other children to take her toys without a struggle, and showed only spasmodic interest in their constructive use. However, there were a few redeeming moments when she showed a good attention span.

After six months of treatment, when she was two years old, Louise was once more put on phenobarbitol sedative to relieve her tension and to reduce her hyperactivity. She was not enjoying the other children in her institution unit, frequently biting and teasing, taking toys, and insisting on getting her own way. She was still jealous of the other children, only occasionally tolerating adult attention to them without flaring up in a temper.

Generally her behaviour in a group was over-excitable. On the other hand, she was accepting adults much better than formerly. While still doing almost anything to get attention, she seemed more ready to believe that they might be concerned about her welfare. She responded to and sought out demonstrations of affection from familiar adults, but would still run away crying from unfamiliar ones. If hurt, she sought out unnecessary adult reassurance. Compulsive behaviour was now being demonstrated in her insistence on turning over all chairs. She constantly twisted her hair and cried a great deal when tired.

On the other hand, she was taking a new experience, the institution nursery school, enthusiastically in her stride. While at the school, her motor restlessness was reflected in strenuous activity which bordered on heedlessness of danger. The general nature of her activity was desultory and her interests skipped rapidly from one thing to another. She was rebellious about rules in the playground and in the nursery school. She often whined and became impatient when encountering difficulties with playthings. Her play was almost totally lacking in constructiveness.

She was generally irresponsible in routines, following out the expected dressing requirements only under constant adult direction. While responding co-operatively to attempts at toilet training, she seemed immature and was generally irregular in her eliminative function. Her enjoyment of eating was reflected in a very large appetite, and her disturbing behaviour at meal times was subsiding. Sleep time remained upset and erratic. Although Louise seemed to require more sleep than many children, she resisted being put to bed with tears and temper tantrums. Once in bed she remained awake for long periods, calling out and getting up to play. If her bed was put in a different room, she would become upset and scream. She clung to a piece of cloth. On the other hand, she co-operated well in the preliminary bed-time preparations, and once asleep, seemed relaxed and slept soundly. She usually woke up cheerful. She now spoke in clear words.

The next three months seemed to bring about improvements in her behaviour. Her physical development improved remarkably. She gained considerable weight and became a large, pretty, well-formed, and sturdy child. Her security score increased to 29. Whereas she had formerly been aggressive with and antagonistic towards other children in her unit, she now seemed able to enjoy them most of the time, recognizing that they had rights to toys and a place in the unit. If overly excited, she would still revert to her habits of biting, pushing, taking the other children's toys, and insisting on her own way.

Louise still had a venturesome attitude towards new experiences; car rides, visits to Santa Claus, and animals were all accepted as part of a new world which she appeared to regard as wonderful. Although her attention span was still very short and her play with toys erratic, there was a great improvement in the quality of her play with materials. She had become genuinely interested in some play materials and could concentrate constructively under close adult supervision. She was still easily frustrated and would throw toys when displeased with them. She frequently argued about rules and restrictions regarding the use of toys, ignoring, disobeying, and sulking when the rules were explained or if she was reminded about them.

Two months previously, shortly after turning two, Louise had acquired volunteer parents who introduced her to many new experiences in the community and in their home. In the two months following her first experience with volunteer parents she began to look forward to her times with them, apparently developing a sense of dependence on them. She would seek them out for comfort and would respond readily to their physical demonstrations of affection. She generally obeyed their instructions, although at times she would be playful and tease or else sulk. She now accepted unfamiliar adults, on initial meeting, and actually seemed to enjoy crowds. She had to be protected from too much social stimulation as she would easily become over-stimulated and resort to erratic and tense behaviour, generally heedless and lacking control and direction.

Her attitude towards routines such as dressing was now one of active interest rather than indifference. She now wanted to dress herself, but needed adult help because she lacked skill. She was generally co-operative about rules during her daily hour in the nursery school. Her toilet training was complete. She continued to relish meals in large quantities and tended to be messy and impatient when feeding herself. Her behaviour at bed time was improving greatly. She was much more co-operative when put to bed, struggling and resisting only when over-tired. She still slept soundly and was generally relaxed, although she would occasionally cry out at night. She twisted her hair while going to sleep.

Her relationship with her volunteer parents affected her behaviour in the institution. Whenever she returned from a visit to them, she seemed irritable, aimless, and aggressive for several days before settling down to the routine of institutional life.

It was at this point that Louise's volunteer parents began to press for adoption. Louise's weekend visits with them were prolonged on two occasions by the sudden onset of illness (cold at one time, measles at another). The relationship seemed to be growing daily closer between them, and finally an adoption study was made of the home. Louise was placed in their home at the age of two years and five months.

After placement, Louise's parents settled comfortably in anticipation of life with a normal little girl. The lovely "honeymoon" period of initial conformity, common with most of the children, reinforced their feeling of confidence in a happy adoption. It was only as Louise began to let down her controls and permit her conflict to reveal itself in an atmosphere where she was fully accepted, that her parents felt a growing apprehension about their ability to live comfortably with her. After six months had elapsed, they finally called Miss Kilgour for assistance.

By this time Louise was two years and eleven months of age, and her score on the pre-school security test revealed a severe decline from her last testing (a drop from 29 to 9). Her behaviour reflected conflict and lack of both inner and outer controls. She seemed bewildered. She was constantly irritable and rebellious, and seemed to have no trust in her parents or other adults. She even refused dependency where she seriously needed it. "Louise do" became a whiney and negative expression of her attitude toward help from her parents.

Her play habits had disintegrated to distractible, hyperactive flitting from one thing to another. She was aimless and lacking in interest or direction. Her old problems in sleeping had recurred. Although exhausted, she would stay awake at night for hours, crying, whining, and generally appearing overly excited. On one occasion her exhausted parents found her asleep on the top of a chest of drawers. She was restless and tense while asleep, and constantly chewed and sucked her blanket. Meal times had deteriorated to an unhappy struggle between parents and child, where her over-excited behaviour constantly interrupted the meal and her over-talkativeness left no opportunity for adult conversation. Her old trouble of constipation had returned.

Her parents were greatly perturbed, and in an effort to give the child more scope to roam about, had started to live a great deal of the time with the maternal grandparents, who had a larger house and garden. An investigation of the whole situation revealed that the parents were unwittingly restraining the child in ways which were frustrating, unreasonable, and incomprehensible to her. Since her placement, she had been the recipient of doting attention from parents, grandparents, and older cousins. Few rules of conduct were established and few controls imposed. Whenever discipline did occur, it sometimes became the subject of disagreement between the mother and grandmother.

There was no real consistency to any of the child's routines, and they were totally failing to meet her need for an orderly, predictable, and comfortable world. Her parents were deeply fond of her, but totally bewildered by her behaviour and helpless to establish a course of action which would make her more happy and secure.

The rather small and expensively furnished apartment in which they lived was a source of pride to them, and the mother's reluctance to cover up some of the decorations in Louise's bedroom and the living room provided a chronic source of nagging between mother and child. Louise's talent for manipulating adults by any means within her grasp had been given full rein. As a result, her parents never felt any sense of easiness or enjoyment in her presence, nor did they feel that discipline made any impression on her. When thwarted, Louise seemed almost beside herself, and her response to direction had a heedless, tense, and distractible quality. She tended to ignore her parent's requests and to go about her own erratic way. Her mother expressed the opinion that "Louise was happy only when getting her own way."

While Miss Kilgour was visiting mother and child, she witnessed an expression of Louise's defiance. Louise darted to a drawer, pulled out her father's socks and tossed them in the air. She darted and picked up plastic dishes, throwing them about the room. In apparent anticipation of an adult "no," she commenced defiantly hiding pieces of a puzzle behind blinds and under the radio. She then sat and looked at a picture book with the visitor, but needed continual redirection to capture her interest. She constantly darted to the radio, turning it off and on. When the telephone rang, she ran to it, picked it up with a chuckle and called, "Hi, Daddy."

On the other hand, there were also certain strengths in Louise's adjustment to her family. Despite her anxiety to be the centre of attention with both adults and children, she was tackling her new world with enthusiasm. She still approached new situations eagerly and with little fear. She was turning to her parents for some assurance and for demonstrations of affection. She was attracted indiscriminately to all adults, to the extent that one questioned the depth of her relationships with anyone. Her tremendous tension was being released in a variety of ways, difficult to watch, but probably valuable to her well-being. Twisting her hair, rocking, biting her nails and her toys, chewing bed-clothes, and chewing and spanking her teddy bear were chronic activities. She was interested in dressing herself, and would pay fairly close attention to that routine. Her toilet habits still remained good, although some regression to bed-wetting had occurred recently. Although distractible and over-talkative at mealtimes, she enjoyed food, was ready to taste new foods, and fed herself fairly well.

Louise's parents were now ready to accept direct help and to follow specific suggestions. Accordingly, the family physician was consulted and sedatives were prescribed. Miss Kilgour and Louise's mother then worked out a specific plan to cover the whole day. Following this plan from day to day was intended to give order and meaning to Louise's life. The parents' readiness to accept this help was reflected in their immediate attempt to employ the new schedule. Both mother and father were able to admit that they had not been ready to listen to any warning or advice six months ago but were now learning what had been meant. Their attitude on interview seemed to be much more considerate of the child's needs than formerly, and they showed a recognition that they must adapt in some instances and at the same time give more direction and control.

By September, at the age of three years and three months, Louise seemed to have progressed to a period during which her behaviour was rewarding. Although her parents still spoke of "on and off days," her general behaviour had become so much easier to live with that they were hopeful of having a relaxed, normal child to enjoy. Their home had become child-centred. Furniture was protected by slip covers, children's toys in toy boxes were allowed in the living room. Definite rules, such as "do not touch the TV," were established, and Louise's mother was anticipating over-excitable and negative behaviour by adroitly avoiding provoking situations which would upset Louise. Irritating habits, formerly the cause of nagging, were being ignored. Social stimulation, particularly exciting to Louise, was kept to a minimum. To establish a closer relationship, her mother gave Louise more help in routines than formerly, and some dependency seemed to develop as a result. Problems gradually diminished during the routines of dressing and using the toilet. Bed-wetting ceased and constipation disappeared. Eating still was difficult, with Louise dawdling and procrastinating, while talking constantly. However, she enjoyed her food and was delighted to be fed by her mother, a system that automatically permitted less nagging about finishing meals. She seemed generally more dependent, clinging and seeking help in nearly all situations. No longer was it "Louise do it," but rather, "Mummy help Louise."

She was still on sedation, and her sleep had improved considerably, so that she now slept fourteen hours a day. Her extreme sociability was waning, and she would first cling to her mother in the presence of strangers. She was showing signs of being an attractive clown and mimic while manipulating people. Tics, such as chewing her bed clothes, masturbating, rocking, and twisting her hair, had ceased, and nail-biting occurred only when she was extremely tired. Her darting, excitable behaviour was diminished. She was less openly defiant, but rather was using the technique of teasing and testing.

She could now amuse herself with her toys. She was seldom destructive with them and would ask for help if frustrated while using them. In her few contacts with children, she was showing a greater ability to be co-operative, and she did not always have to be the "boss." Given a choice, she would choose older children whom she could manipulate with her winsome ways in order to gain attention.

Things seemed for a while to be improving for Louise and her parents, but gradually the closer dependency established between them showed signs of increasing the tension and irritability among them. While contributing to Louise's self-confidence, the relationship was becoming more difficult for her mother, as she was being constantly teased and tested. For this reason nursery school for a few hours a week seemed to offer hope of reducing such tense interaction between mother and child, and also to offer an opportunity to continue the development of good play habits and supervised social play with Louise's contemporaries.

A small nursery school with a large staff capable of giving a lot of individual help was found and Louise was very gradually introduced to this new experience. Her reaction revealed again her lack of well-integrated development. For the first few days, she was enthusiastic and eager for nursery school, but on returning home was overly excited and highly stimulated. A week after she had started, Louise had regressed so seriously in her behaviour that withdrawal was contemplated. She was erratic and disobedient. She started getting up in the middle of the night, taking off her clothes, and running into the kitchen. Once she got up yelling, screaming, and banging doors at three A.M. and wet her pyjamas twice. Both parents remarked that the child "appears to enjoy thoroughly the fact that she is defiant and apparently controlling her environment." She was now refusing to go to nursery school.

Two weeks later, the storm seemed to be over. Her behaviour returned to its normal state at home, and her adjustment to nursery school seemed adequate. She participated enthusiastically in all activities and showed little sign of her old distractibility. She was liked by the children and staff, had no sign of tics, and was showing an increased attention span in her use of play materials. In the following months, she settled into nursery school activity with enthusiasm and seemed to benefit from her contact with both the staff and the children. She accepted direction from the staff and seemed to be learning that aggressive behaviour with her contemporaries reaped few rewards. She showed persistence with play materials, but still needed to be protected from over-stimulation. Too much social interaction would still precipitate distractible and erratic behaviour even in this controlled setting.

At home, child and parents seemed to grow closer. There was recognition and acceptance of Louise's shortcomings. "You can do anything with her through love and affection, but the minute you push her she is as stubborn and determined as a mule," her parents said. If her life was highly controlled and carefully planned, Louise moved happily and relatively normally through her days. Under stress or unusual circumstances which required an adjustment of her routine, Louise degenerated to distractibility and defiance. Her general personality was one of an aggressive, hyperactive charmer, difficult to live with but also a great deal of fun. She was lovable, determined, and saucy. She seemed to have made great advances in her intellectual functioning and appeared above average in her vocabulary and in her ability to reason and relate experiences to one another.

Adoption was finalized for Louise when she was three and a half years of age. Although she could now remain off sedatives, no one, including her parents, anticipated that life would ever be easy with Louise. It appeared from her past behaviour that she would always be particularly vulnerable to stress, and for this reason would need more than the usual recognition of her emotional needs.

14

Harry

SECURITY SCORES

Age	Score[*]
10 months	+0.39
11 months	+0.11
12 months	+0.18
13 months	+0.10
14 months	+0.03
3 years	11
3 years 3 months	5
3 years 9 months	−4
3 years 11 months	−7
4 years 2 months	18
4 years 5 months	29
4 years 9 months	35
5 years	26

[*]Scores for ages under two years are from the Infant Security Scale. All other scores are from Pre-school Mental Health Assessment Form.

HARRY was a tense, anxious boy when we first had the opportunity to observe him closely at ten months of age. His behaviour at this time indicated that he was within a normal range of mental health; his infant security score was approximately that of normal babies (18). Thereafter he was observed monthly for five months, during which time his behaviour gradually deteriorated and reflected marked insecurity, becoming progressively worse each month. Harry was not observed again until the following year when, for six months, he was exposed to the experimental playroom under the supervision of Miss Kilgour and her assistant. Here, with constant direction, and while in the playroom with one adult and no children, he demonstrated his ability to make profitable use of play materials despite nearly two years of barren institutional upbringing. His activity with the toys was so far superior to that of the other children under the same circumstances that he was judged to be of rather high intelligence—certainly he seemed to have greater ability than the other children in the institution.

Harry was not observed again until the rehabilitation programme was well established and he was three years of age. At this time, his security score was very low (11 on the pre-school scale). He was demonstrating characteristics similar to those seen when he was an infant. He was torn by conflict, wanting to go out to his world but apparently fearful that it would be unrewarding. He was assertive, unpleasant, and aggressive, with both adults and children. He seemed determined to make his presence felt in any possible way and was evidently putting up tremendous resistance to the inroads of institutional life. During the following year he continued to fight his world, overtly expressing his anxiety. Unlike many of the other children, he seemed determined not to succumb to lethargy. As a result, his expressed turmoil and conflict continued to create an uncomfortable disturbance wherever he went.

It was not until he was four and a half years of age that he began to show signs of lessened insecurity. However, he still dominated the scene by asserting himself in either an ingratiating or an aggressive way. One constantly had the feeling that Harry saw himself as a unique person and was determined that nothing could reduce him to the status of just "one of the crowd." He was so aggressive that he could never be lost or forgotten in a group. His needs were always made known. He was so consistently "the big me" that his dominating, organizing behaviour with the other children finally brought about the necessity of his having his own room. In order to dominate the situation further, he insisted on having his full name on the door. With this added boost to his ego, he began to be somewhat comfortable within the institution, and his security score increased to 35. Through his experiences in the home of a volunteer, and as a result of seeing many of the other children going to foster and adoptive homes where they acquired their own mother and father, he began reaching anxiously beyond the institution, demanding, "When can I go away and never come back?"

After many months of careful searching, a home was found through one of the volunteers with professional people who wanted a "challenge" in their adoptive child. On hearing that a mother and father had been found who wanted him, Harry was beside himself with anxiety. When could he leave the institution and go to his own new home? After two visits, returning to the institution was so upsetting for Harry that it was decided he should forego the usual careful pre-visiting and should go to his new home immediately. Despite their enthusiasm, his prospective parents were obviously unready for the introduction of this overwhelming little boy to their home. No amount of explanation could replace some of the living experiences which would be necessary before they could clearly see the extent of the challenge he presented to them. Therefore, close guidance was initiated after placement in his adoptive home. When the inevitable "honeymoon" period was over, the problems began to arise and his grateful parents willingly shared their experiences with Miss Kilgour, who helped work out a step-by-step plan to ease both the family and Harry over the turmoil of fitting into a new life.

The story of Harry's response to treatment in the institution is uniquely *his* story. He was a child of such strongly marked personality characteristics that he required more thought and attention to the satisfaction of his immediate demands than many of the other children. For this reason also, he seemed to have more to offer of both intellectual endowment and richness of personality than many of the other children.

When the treatment programme began in February 1958, Harry, aged three years three months, was a handsome, attractive, and aggressive child. Although his behaviour gave indications of relatively high intelligence, it was felt that a mental test at this early time would yield no accurate estimate. He was most eager to learn and took every opportunity to ask questions. However, he constantly fought for adult attention: screaming, biting, running about erratically, and having violent temper tantrums when other children were given attention instead of himself. His unrest was further expressed in a constantly fierce expression and in insistence on having his own way whenever he was thwarted. Once given the attention of an adult, he would subside and become eagerly co-operative. He made excellent use of play materials, but needed the constant attention of an adult by his side to sustain his capacity for concentration. He generally fought with the other children, attempting to assert himself most of the time. He ate well and his behaviour was acceptable at the table. No difficulties were being encountered in toilet training. Not so his bedtime routine, which he seemed to resent. He always protested going to bed. Once put there, he would often get out screaming and crying and would run up the halls. At other times he would rock and cry.

Once the treatment programme was under way, Harry set out to test the limits of imposed controls. Rather than showing improvement, his behaviour deteriorated further and his security score declined steadily for the next eleven months. Each area of his life now seemed to present a greater opportunity for him to demonstrate his conflict.

By the time he was three years and eleven months of age, his self-control had reached an unprecedented low. He had been sent to a community nursery school as part of an effort to broaden his life experiences and prepare the way for possible future placement in a home. In the nursery school, he seemed quite incapable of making use of any of his suspected latent ability. Rather, he had become so highly distractible and aggressive that one teacher was required for him alone, to keep him under control. He made no constructive use of play materials, going erratically from one toy to another, or destroying them. He was incapable of becoming part of any group activity and was causing such turmoil among the other children that he disrupted the school programme. The many occasions when he had to be thwarted were teaching him nothing, but seemed rather to be building more resistance to adult direction and to school rules. Furthermore, they were creating more situations in which he could express hostility towards adults.

Harry's relationship to adults generally was still poor. While having no real affectionate ties, he made excessive and insistent demands for their attention. If specific demands were not met immediately, he would argue, protest, scream, sulk, hit out, pinch, or spit. He constantly looked sullen and cross. He generally avoided the other children unless he could dominate and threaten them. His inner anxiety showed up in many other ways. He tended to avoid venturesome play and was anxious and fearful of animals. He played aimlessly outdoors and was less able to concentrate on a plaything than before. He would become frustrated by the simplest puzzle, expecting an adult to do it for him. One of the few good aspects to his play was his capacity for imaginative use of his mind.

Dressing provided an opportunity for refusal and arguments. Harry would not allow an unfamiliar person to assist with his clothing. He insisted on wearing what *he* wanted. In the dining room, his voice and noise made things uncomfortable for others. He even made unnecessary demands for assistance in going to the toilet—he would refuse to go when expected, and would argue and postpone the time to go. He was overly interested in his stools. Bedtime was still a miserable routine, fraught with resistance and argument, usually ending up with Harry having a temper tantrum and sleeping by himself. When going to sleep, he sucked his thumb and rocked; if left alone, he seemed disturbed by darkness or a closed door.

Staff consultation about Harry led to several changes in treatment.

He was withdrawn from nursery school because it offered him nothing that he needed at the moment. His living arrangements within the institution were changed and he was placed in a new unit of five children only (the smallest number possible with the given facilities), with a housemother he knew but had not been close to. Each day he was given an hour to play in a permissive setting with a friendly adult. It was hoped that these play sessions might drain off some of his hostility and provide one person whom he could trust for understanding and acceptance. It would also give him some of the individual adult attention which he craved so intensely. To satisfy this need further, his volunteer mother took him out or to her home for half a day each week.

Over the next three months Harry's behaviour showed marked improvement, reflected in a rise of his pre-school security score from —7 to 18. The permissive play sessions with one staff member seemed to help him relax, and his relationship towards other adults showed progressive gains. After six weeks of daily individual play sessions, he seemed ready to take on a limited attendance in the resident nursery school as long as the play groups remained small. For a month he attended the nursery school for three days weekly. The other two days he continued with his play sessions. At the end of this time, he was coping sufficiently with people and events, and play sessions were dropped, five days a week being devoted to nursery school. His relationship with his volunteer mother seemed to be helping him in many ways, and he was occasionally permitted to visit overnight at her home. His volunteer mother was particularly good as a means of broadening his life experiences, while at the same time controlling his behaviour with a firm hand. Through her he learned how people lived in homes, how they dressed, went to church, played, and worked.

He seemed to be developing some genuine affection for his unit mother and talked about her and with her a great deal. Gradually, he was able to accept her firm but kindly discipline and control. There was also some evidence of self-control appearing. His old anxiety in the presence of adults was being replaced by some enjoyment. Now, rather than constantly interrupting conversation and demanding attention, he sought adults for support of his activities and would respond to physical demonstrations of affection. Now, even though refusing direction and frequently argumentative, he could be reasoned with, and would finally become mellow and agreeable. No longer overly aggressive with strange adults, he was now sensitive enough to be anxious and withdrawing.

Harry was also beginning to enjoy the other children, and he even had a special friend. He would accept sharing the attention of his beloved unit mother with the other children; he could share toys and he no longer disrupted his play with other children by stubbornly insisting on his own way. He showed flashes of occasional solicitude towards the other children and found satisfaction through dominating them in a healthy way (e.g., getting a glass of water for a sick child). He still needed to brag and confirm his superiority by stories about his wonderful volunteer. His mind seemed more agile than those of his unit companions, his speech was clearer, he talked more, and was never at a loss for an explanation, whether from his fertile imagination or from fact.

Many of Harry's anxieties seemed to be on the wane. His fear of animals was subsiding, mainly because his volunteer mother had brought him into contact with some animals. He would quickly recover from hurts after being reassured by adult comforting. He looked forward eagerly to new experiences in the community and accepted them with enthusiasm as long as he was accompanied by a trusted adult. He loved everyday experiences at his nursery school. He was cautious about indulging in strenuous physical play, but was learning to enjoy more different kinds of play. His enjoyment of toys and books was reflected in a greatly increased span of attention. Although still impatient when faced with a difficult task, he could wait for adult help and could accept direction.

Harry's behaviour regarding dressing, using the toilet, and eating showed marked improvement. Although he continued to dawdle, talk too much, and ask for unnecessary help in dressing, he could manage these routines without any emotional crises. He still enjoyed nice clothes but was no longer unreasonably resentful about the ones he did not like. He was taking advantage of his responsibilities for using the toilet, and here there was no difficulty. He continued to dawdle and play in the dining room, but could be directed and controlled so he did not disrupt the others. Bed time was fairly enjoyable now that Harry was co-operative. He now could permit a strange staff member to put him to bed. He was more able to relax, sucking his fingers and droning before falling off to sleep. He remained a light sleeper but was no longer disturbed by darkness or a closed door.

Over the next six or seven months, Harry showed such marked improvement in his behaviour that every effort was directed towards finding an adoptive family who could control this difficult child and at the same time encourage the unfolding of his intellectual potential and whatever capacity he had for warm emotional expression. Finally, through his volunteer mother, parents were found who were interested in having a "challenge" in their adopted child. They lived eighty miles from the institution in a small town where they had considerable status.

Prior to placement, they had observed Harry at a social gathering where he was unaware of their interest in him. After their decision to adopt him, they came to the institution for a visit and a discussion regarding Harry. In order to give them some tangible information, Harry's qualities, both good and bad, were discussed with them. It was pointed out that in view of Harry's past, difficulties would be encountered, and it would be essential that the parents accept some direction and guidance from professional workers who knew him best.

At this point in Harry's life, he was an alert, enthusiastic, dominating, and endearing child. He was obviously still anxious to prove his worth, and with unfamiliar persons he could be expected to establish a sense of his importance by manipulating them in any possible way. If all else failed, he could be relied upon to resort to screaming, fighting, and tantrums to get his own way. However, if he felt loved and accepted, his belligerence would melt into an attitude of sweet reasonableness, whereby he could listen to and accept explanations of the purpose behind discipline and adult control. Although he was still desperately averse to "losing face" with his friends, both adults and children, he would try to divert them with tenderness and thoughtfulness rather than admit he might be wrong. With familiar people guiding him, he was capable of exercising considerable self-control. He had a lively intelligence which was searching for satisfactions beyond those supplied by life in the institution. He thought constructively, trying to establish some order and reason to his life by many "why" questions. His activity was no longer aimless. He was interested in his whole expanding world, and he absorbed many experiences vicariously through books, which he constantly wanted read to him.

He loved to appear capable of handling any experience which might come his way. He seemed satisfied only when he fully understood all factors regarding any situation involving himself. His goals for himself were very high and caused him much anxiety about his ability to achieve them. He was particularly sensitive to the implication of any social situation and felt called upon to make a good impression. He was still capable of getting keyed up and out of control in a group of people. He could sense the opportune moment to gain his own ends with people.

It was suggested to his adopting parents that Harry's bed time be planned very carefully and that he should be made to carry out the routine consistently, with no deviation. Under these circumstances, he could settle to sleep comfortably. If the routine were not adhered to, or if a stranger were in charge of the bedtime routine, he could become highly excited and test the limits to the point of desperation. Mealtime was generally pleasant, and the toilet and dressing routines presented no problems.

Harry's placement was the culmination of many months of anxiety on his part. His quick intelligence and sensitivity to what was going on around him had made him intensely aware that some of the other children had found parents and had moved away to homes. "Why is Father Stone taking so long to get me a mommy and daddy?" "So many people in this house go away and never come back. Now Cochrane has gone away." His weekend activities and summer holidays with his volunteer parents made him sensitive to the advantage of life in a family, with its unique capacity to satisfy most of his needs and particularly to cater to his unusual and rather aggressive personality.

Through his volunteer family he was brought in contact with his future parents. When adoption was decided on, he was told that a mother and father had been found. He anxiously expressed a desire to go immediately to his new home. Because of his anxiety and the fact that his new home was a two-hour drive from the institution, the normal carefully planned and prolonged pre-placement visits were waived. Harry was obviously finding the institution more and more restrictive, and he resented being encapsulated there. Many small things were done to make Harry feel the reassurance that his future home would not evaporate as a dream.

The day he was told about his new parents, he went to dinner with them. They bought him a raincoat and a bedspread for his future bed. He was reassured that despite his parents' going on a holiday, they would write him every day and telephone him. This promise was kept. On their return from their holiday, Harry visited his parents in his new home. Throughout the visit he seemed composed and eager to stay. He slept for an hour in his new bedroom, looked forward to the future by asking if he was to have new curtains, and seemed to feel that this was certainly *his* home. So eager was he to remain that it was thought he could not benefit by any more pre-placement visits. He returned to the institution with the family suitcase. He had one day to pack his bag and sever his connection with his friends in this building which had been the core of his life for nearly five years.

Whatever help he might need to adjust to his new home would be given after placement.

Harry expressed no regrets on leaving the institution. Even his beloved unit mother, for whom he had seemingly had deep feeling, received little demonstration of affection. While his unit mother silently wept on their parting, he gave her a hug, wholly intent on his immediate journey and the wonder of his new home. The two-hour trip provided scope for Harry's mounting anxiety. The first hour and a quarter was uneventful. Harry seemed content to look at books and eat jelly beans. Then his restlessness increased, and finally his anxiety was expressed. "Don't get lost.... If you go the wrong way, I won't live. I won't have a daddy." "I don't like the sun in my eyes." "I have a tummy ache." "Oh, my, I don't feel very well." When given a watch to count the minutes until he arrived, he relaxed a bit and chatted about the broken TV set his new father had, the chipmunk in the garden, and his mother. On arrival, Harry ran to meet his parents and then darted to his bedroom to assure himself that his new curtains were up. He showed his mother the precious possessions he had brought with him from the institution, and after his parents had gone to the living room to talk with Miss Kilgour, he remained in his bedroom, investigating every detail. He showed delight in his new pyjamas and dressing gown. Afterwards, sitting in the kitchen, he confirmed his permanence by stating, "This is where I will always eat and sit—this will be my chair." When put to bed for his afternoon nap, he was happy to have his mother take off his shoes. As an afterthought, he ran to the living room to say good-bye to Miss Kilgour, and went back to his bed, happily rocking and talking to himself.

Thus ended one phase of Harry's life, and a new one began. This outgoing, appealing child, with a capacity for tenderness and a need to belong to someone whom he could trust, could prove rewarding and charming, given the kind of treatment and enriched environment which would make use of his capacity, and the firmness of adult direction and control which would prevent him from using people only as a means to an end. His new parents seemed willing to accept help from Miss Kilgour with their difficulties, but felt capable of coping adequately with Harry on most issues. The story of his adjustment and the final outcome of his placement must await final study. At present, we believe that this will be one of the most successful of the adoption placements. "The big me" who swaggered about the institution should develop into a rewarding youngster with a capacity to do well in school and to fit well into the community.

PART FOUR · CONCLUSIONS

15

The Cost of Care and the Saving
to the Community

THE COST of caring for children who have no family or guardians has always been a major community problem. In Ontario, the Child Welfare Act makes provisions for the protection and maintenance of children who are found to be neglected under the provisions of the Act. By court order, a child may be made a ward of a Children's Aid Society, and the cost of maintenance assessed against the municipality involved, on the basis of the average daily cost to the Society for the maintenance of the children in its care.

The institution described in this study was operated by the Catholic Children's Aid Society of Metropolitan Toronto, and was used for the accommodation of infants who were wards of the Society. The cost of the maintenance of the children was borne by the Municipality of Metropolitan Toronto.

When the change was to be made from an institutional residence to a treatment centre, it was evident that greatly increased costs of operation were involved. The Municipality was approached, and gave its endorsement to the project and its approval of the increases in budget to cover the extra costs. Table I shows the operating costs of the institution for the years 1957 through 1960. It reflects the progress of the project through its various phases. During the four years a total of $528,499.59 was spent. By the end of that period the majority of the children had been placed in either foster or adoptive homes. A few who were hopelessly retarded had been sent even before the end of the first year to Provincial institutions for the care of seriously defective persons. Because most of the placements were to adoptive homes, the cost was lifted from the community and placed on the private resources of the adoptive family.

The figure of $528,499.59 must be regarded as a rough estimate, as there were also hidden costs: costs of agency administration, incidental casework expenses, and costs of the clothing supplied by volunteers.

TABLE I

	Daily rate		
Year	per child	total operation	Yearly rate, total operation
1957	$ 4.19	$327.97	$119,709.61
1958	8.26	488.22	178,201.44
1959	9.76	368.03	134,331.42
1960	13.81	263.44	96,257.12
Total			$528,499.59

Table II shows the number of children receiving care from 1957 to 1960 inclusive.

TABLE II

	In residence			Average daily population
Year	Jan. 1	Dec. 31	Total days of care per child	(total days of care/365)
1957	83	73	28,591	78.3
1958	73	49	21,581	59.1
1959	49	29	13,762	37.7
1960	29	9	6,986	19.1

From the tables it is evident that the third and fourth years of operating the treatment centre were the most costly per child. This was due in part to the nature of the children still in care. The first group of children who responded fairly readily to treatment had been moved on to homes. Those who remained were more seriously damaged children who needed much more intensive work requiring a large ratio of staff members per child.

The figures seem high and indicate why it is often difficult to obtain sufficient money from a community to improve an institution to the level of a treatment centre. However, it is easy to demonstrate that on a long-term basis the cost to the community is comparatively small. Whereas over a period of four years the cost of operation was roughly $528,499.59, had the children remained in care for 18 years, as have most institutionalized children in the past, the cost would have been much greater.

The average daily amount paid by the Municipality to care for each child was $3.08. (See Table III.)

TABLE III

Year	Rate
1957	$2.76
1958	3.35
1959	2.90
1960	3.33
Average	$3.08

Let us assume that the 83 children in care at the beginning of 1957 would not have been placed in foster homes, nor could they have gone to adoption (a reasonable assumption, since most children become non-placeable after a few months of institutional life). By remaining in the institution as a ward of the state and requiring support from the municipality for 18 years, they would cost the community a minimum of $1,679,554.80. (83 children × 365 days = 30,295 days of care yearly; 18 years × 30,295 days = 545,310 days of care; cost for 545,310 days of care at $3.08 per day = $1,679,554.80.)

This figure does not take into consideration the rising cost of care which would inevitably take place over a period of 18 years. Nor does it consider all the extra cost which these children are known to incur during a lifetime of moving from one institution to another. It is acknowledged that special services arising from delinquent acts, court hearings, damages to the community, psychiatric guidance, and even incarceration would be added to this cost. The total might be slightly reduced by an occasional child who would be returned to his own parents, and a few who might go to foster homes and later to adoptive care. But it can be seen that the long-term care of children left untreated in an institution would have been at least three times as great as the short-term treatment programme designed to restore the children to normal mental health.

Table IV shows a breakdown of the operating costs of the McNeil Home from 1957 to 1960 inclusive. It can be seen that the largest amount of money was spent on salaries ($421,420.20), since a successful programme requires a high staff-to-child ratio. Another costly part of the programme came from renovation and repairs to the building. Tearing down partitions, putting in extra bathrooms, installing playrooms, revamping the kitchen, and remodelling an old coach house for a nursery school cost roughly $20,187.39. These steps were considered essential environmental changes to enable the treatment centre to operate successfully.

TABLE IV
BREAKDOWN OF OPERATING COSTS
1957 TO 1960 INCLUSIVE

	1957	1958	1959	1960	Total for four years
Salaries	$84,841.99	$144,471.26	$113,852.05	$78,354.90	$421,420.20
Food	19,515.43	10,545.50	7,038.22	4,915.95	41,135.84
Laundry	1,161.21	1,643.29	1,212.22	688.64	4,710.56
Medical supplies	1,617.95	1,265.12	743.59	546.75	4,173.41
Recreation facilities	305.88	47.87	4.92	9.70	368.37
Special needs	8.14	41.65	222.15	122.20	394.14
Insurance	48.90	85.00	86.40	86.60	306.90
Light, heat, water	4,456.82	3,879.75	3,649.04	3,024.03	15,009.64
Cleaning and maintenance supplies	1,692.06	3,442.40	1,983.37	1,252.32	8,370.15
Repairs to building	2,842.31	9,337.22	2,804.50	5,203.36	20,187.39
Renewal of furniture	367.58	1,144.76	465.52	98.73	2,076.59
Depreciation of equipment	2,478.39	1,814.00	1,613.76	1,301.01	7,207.16
Telephone	295.95	465.34	554.55	603.30	1,819.14
Sundry	77.00	118.28	95.39	49.63	340.30
Total	$119,709.61	$178,201.44	$134,331.42	$96,257.12	$528,499.51

16

Some Thoughts on Institutional Care

WE HAVE LEARNED a great deal since the children from the McNeil Home were first placed. One phenomenon that became evident was that behaviour could approximate normality in the protected environment of the treatment centre, while feelings of adequacy and a true understanding of the demands of adults and the rules of conduct lagged behind, both in the institution and in homes. Furthermore, we have had to face the disappointment of recognizing that the course of normal development is not inevitably furthered by well-meaning foster or adoptive parents. The needs and aspirations of parents, often unrecognized and certainly not spoken, often limit rather than foster a child's potential. This limitation frequently does not appear in the first six months to a year after placement, but becomes evident after the parents have promoted healthy development to the point where the child appears to have settled into his home with some confidence and is ready to assert himself as an individual. The case histories of 31 of these children after placement will be reported elsewhere in journal articles (44) and will be further expanded in another book.

Conclusions

The treatment programme described here confirmed some of the expectations we had held at the beginning, but the response of some of the children to therapy provided many surprises. The programme demonstrated the degree to which children with greatly differing personalities can respond to an enriched and benign environment, and it revealed the intensity of their needs for adults who care for them. It further demonstrated their capacity to reach out for and consolidate a relationship with adults once given an opportunity, and it taught us how to make individual adaptations within a large framework in order to meet the needs of each child most adequately. A variety of methods of staff training were employed and assessed. Together with constant supervisory guidance and some new insight into the world of a child, they gave new capacity and strength to a formerly untrained staff.

We had anticipated that the youngest children with the least institutional experience would respond most quickly and make the most adequate recovery in the group. Essentially that is what happened. Given an opportunity to build a dependent relationship with an interested and constant staff member, the youngest children demonstrated a reassuring capacity to empathize and communicate with others. With their dependency consolidated in one or two individuals, they emerged from their self-preoccupation to demand more attention, more activity, and more space in which to live. The well-being arising from whatever trusting dependency they could achieve led them to reach out beyond this initial relationship to other people and other interests. A few months after treatment was begun, some of the youngsters were showing sufficient healthy symptoms to be considered ready for placement in homes.

We had not anticipated that the older children, who had suffered deprivation for periods of two and a half to four years, would show swift response to treatment. That they did so amazed us. These inarticulate, undeveloped youngsters who had formed no relationships in their lives, who were aimless and without a capacity to concentrate on anything, had resembled a pack of animals more than a group of human beings. We had predicted a long and disappointing period of treatment before there would be any adequate response at all. As we worked with the children, it became apparent that their inadequacy was not the result of "damage," but rather was due to a dearth of normal experiences without which the development of human qualities is impossible. When affection was displayed towards them, consistent care given, and encouragement offered in such activities as eating, dressing, and washing, they responded with surprising intensity. They seemed to yearn insatiably for adult contacts and attention. Their first response to treatment was to demand relationships, but they had little capacity to respond humanly to attention and little willingness to accept controls. Although it was apparent that they would respond to treatment much more rapidly than we had anticipated, they would, of course, take longer to recover than the younger children.

After a year of treatment, many of these older children were showing a trusting dependency toward staff and volunteers, and in view of their degree of self-reliance in play and routines, seemed to be developing feelings of self-trust. Apathetic behaviour had almost disappeared from the McNeil Home; instead there was direction and purpose to the children's activity. This extreme change in behaviour seemed miraculous and probably made the staff and supervisors overly optimistic about their advancement toward sound mental health. We knew that the children seemed more self-confident and in control of themselves within the protective framework of the treatment centre than they would be living in the community where more demands would be put on them to act like children their own age. We suspected that they would be vulnerable to pressures of normal living, but we could not anticipate the degree to which this might be true.

Furthermore, placement of these children in homes was complicated by their age. Most families wishing to take children for foster and adoptive care prefer a baby rather than a child of even one year. Therefore we had to seek parents who had particular needs of their own which might be met by children of over two and three years of age. Beyond this, the parents must be able to understand the confusion, the longings, the loneliness, and the deviations of children whose background would inevitably make them different from other children in their community. In order to achieve the most satisfactory placement, each child needed to be given a home where his unique qualities could be fostered and his peculiar behaviour tolerated. Ultimate success of rehabilitation would depend largely upon the degree to which parents could relinquish many of their own aspirations and fondest hopes in order to meet the rather unique needs of their special child. This could only come after the reality of living with the child had been experienced.

To compensate for these difficulties and promote every possible success in placement, a social worker who had long experience with children in institutional care was added to the staff of the McNeil Home. She and Miss Kilgour interviewed most of the prospective parents and effected the transfer of the children from the institution to their new families. The transition from the institution to home was usually prolonged in an attempt to permit each child to understand the nature of the change and, hopefully, to alert the parents to the particular qualities and problems of the child with whom they were choosing to live. Where there were already children in the home, the gradual introduction also allowed them some acquaintance with the new child. There were usually five to eight pre-placement visits to a new home, including weekend visits. Following placement, close contact was kept with the parents and child in order to encourage, advise, and support the new relationship. Miss Kilgour usually carried this responsibility, because it was she who had known the child best for the longest time. Daily telephone calls, as well as frequent visits, were quite usual.

Research

An unusual aspect of these placements was the expectation that the parents should keep research records, give information to Miss Kilgour in interviews, and bring the children to the Institute of Child Study for follow-up interviews and for intellectual and personality assessments at given times in the future. Furthermore, they were expected to permit Miss Kilgour to obtain information regarding school achievement and general adjustment from the schools which the children would be attending. Each parent was acquainted with the idea that the treatment centre had a two-fold purpose, one of which was to rehabilitate deprived youngsters, and the second of which was to carry out research on the effectiveness of treatment and the response of each child to it. The importance of long-term follow-up of the children's adjustment to home and community was emphasized. The parent recognized that the research was being conducted not by the Catholic Children's Aid Society, but by the Institute of Child Study, which had been responsible for the research aspect of the treatment programme from its inception. Once the children were in homes, Miss Kilgour's role assumed a dual aspect: that of confidant and guide, and that of data collector. Fortunately her training had equipped her for both duties, and she had constant support in them from the staff of the Institute of Child Study. Later, her dual role was formalized by a double appointment from both the Society and the Institute.

The dual role was obviously an excellent arrangement both for the promotion of optimum adjustment and for the collection of a large amount of information about the children's adaptation to their new environment. Miss Kilgour's constant readiness to advise, to interpret feelings and behaviour to parents (28), to anticipate difficulties and prevent them from overwhelming the new families, and to seek extra community help when it was needed undoubtedly contributed largely to the success of many placements and enriched our understanding about them.

Record-keeping had always been part of the staff duties in the treatment centre. Its main purpose was to collect some systematic data for research purposes. The Infant Security Scale and the Pre-school Mental Health Assessment Form which had been developed at the

Institute of Child Study, although still in an experimental stage, provided a profitable and relatively simple way to accumulate information, both of the forms being behaviour rating scales. Each child's behaviour was recorded routinely every three months. In addition, information was carefully recorded concerning programme changes and their purpose, the short-term progress or regression of each child, the physical condition of individuals and their special treatment, volunteer records, and notations about any special events in a child's life.

Keeping accurate records posed several problems. The first year in the treatment centre was so busy, and so many changes took place, that the staff felt pressed and harassed attending to practical duties with the children, and were often disgruntled by the necessity to stop for recording. However, the collection of data proved valuable in several ways other than merely as an accumulation of information. Despite the difficulty for staff-in-training to keep records, the necessity for them to do so helped them look carefully at each child and achieve a higher degree of objectivity than would have been possible otherwise. The fact that actual behaviour was recorded permitted staff discussion of its meaning, and gave insight into the ways behaviour reflected underlying feelings and indicated degrees of mental health. It also made us alert to the facts that superficial conformity to expected behaviour patterns could precede true underlying improvement in mental health and that ideally one must look for stable behaviour of a type which indicates the individual's real feelings. This integration of behaviour and feeling would be reflected in the consistency with which the same items appeared on the behaviour rating scales over a period of time.

As mentioned earlier, the research records offered an excellent method of noting each child's progress or regression. Furthermore, the reaction of a total group to the programme was reflected in the records and afforded a cross-sectional appraisal which reflected strengths and weaknesses of the total programme and indicated matters which needed to be rectified.

As one by one the children showed sufficient signs of improvement to be moved out of the institution and we could anticipate the final closing of its doors, our assessment of the successes and failures of the total experiment made us question the premise that institutional care for young children need inevitably be damaging to mental health. Certainly, we could point to many positive assets in the McNeil Home as its programme evolved and became increasingly adequate to fill the needs of young children. In view of the continuing requirement for institutional care for young children in our communities, we saw the need to be aware of those aspects which can be cultivated for the promotion of healthy development, as well as those which devastate normal growth. Although we continued to hold to the premise that care in homes is the most salutary environment for young children, we began to believe that institutional care could promote mental health if certain conditions and attitudes prevailed.

Individuality

We concluded that four important principles must be maintained if an institution is to promote healthy development. The first quality which must be recognized and catered to is the uniqueness of each child. From the first few weeks of life on, each child makes its own demands on and response to the world which cares for him. The recognition, acceptance, and encouragement of this particular relationship should be the concern of each staff member who cares for a child. In practice this means that the staff, as a group, must observe, evaluate, and discuss the behaviour of each child, so that unsophisticated workers and observers may see and understand his special qualities. Many environmental symbols must emphasize this uniqueness. Such things as individual clothes, bed-covers, toys, toothbrushes, combs and brushes, cupboards, beds, drawers for possessions, and a particular place in a dining room, bedroom, or playroom all lend a feeling of self-importance to a growing child. The operation of an institution in such a way as to recognize each child's individuality within the group is difficult. Uniformity of treatment erases the necessity for thought, and to impose a group pattern on each child seems the easiest way to operate. Therefore it is essential that the principle of uniqueness be clearly enunciated over and over to staff members working in such a setting.

Dependent Relationships

The second principle which must be kept to the forefront is that mental health in young children can thrive only within the framework of human relationships. Mental health is fostered in an infant by the sympathetic and dependable relationship established by a mothering agent. The feeling of dependent trust which gives an infant reassurance that the world is benign and that care will be forthcoming when it is needed is the basis for all mental health; without it a zest for living cannot develop. It is, therefore, fundamental to the success of an institution that sufficient staff be available to permit a special relationship to develop between a child and one or two selected staff members who are uniquely "his." This sometimes requires extensive juggling of timetables, inconvenience over weekends, and a variety of other measures which are unpopular with staff members.

Initiative

The third principle, which follows on the second, is that children must have an opportunity to expend effort. Channels are usually provided through the opportunity for initiative in taking care of themselves and through effort put into play with things and people. Given sufficient care and attention to establish a feeling of dependent trust, a child will logically move forward in his feeling of well-being to a desire to put forth an effort which is rewarding in itself through the dual satisfactions of enjoyment of activity and of achieving a goal. The environment, therefore, must offer the opportunity to experience rewarding activities both in the form of play and in the routines of feeding oneself, dressing, bathing, and using the toilet. Such activities can be reinforced by an interested adult who gives approval to a child's effort, resulting in self-confidence, one of the essential characteristics of a mentally healthy individual.

Consistency

The fourth principle required for proper development is consistency of care and discipline as practised by the variety of people who look after a child in the period of a day, a week, a month, or a year. Only with a consistent environment can a child build a feeling of a dependable world in which he can predict the consequences of his behaviour as he acts and grows in the course of daily living. It is this predictable aspect of life which gives order and meaning to his actions and the actions of those about him, and enables him to cope adequately with the demands of group life either in a family or in the community. In practice, consistency of handling by a wide variety of people is one of the most difficult things for any staff to achieve. Each individual with his strengths and weaknesses provides a variety of attitudes, tolerances, likes, and dislikes which can only be overcome by constant staff training and the discussion of individual children, their needs, and the way of best meeting these needs. Ideally, such training should be co-ordinated by a central philosophy which gives meaning to the practices and techniques of dealing with the children, and which can be constantly kept in the forefront when staff members discuss methods. Agreement should be achieved on discipline, its meaning to the staff, and its immediate and long-term aims. Only in this way will consistency be approached by a group of people.

Can such conditions be achieved? In institutions which look after children who come from hospitals shortly after birth, such a four-fold plan could provide a salutary environment which would pose no real difficulty in the development of mentally healthy youngsters. Given the opportunity to form relationships with adults who can give consistent care and demonstrate interest, a young child should develop a feeling of self-worth and a reassurance that the world is benign. The desire to put forth effort to do things and to further relationships should inevitably follow, and if plenty of opportunity is provided for a child to be effortful and to extend his horizons as he grows older, he should develop within the range of normal mental health.

A more serious problem is posed by those children who come to institutions from broken homes. In such cases, family break-down or the death of a parent has resulted in a lack of adequate maternal care which is complicated by the shock of losing a parent and all the other familiar environmental ties. A somewhat similar problem is present with young children who come from their own homes to hospitals or to treatment centres for physical therapy or correction of hearing difficulties, or to schools for special training, such as schools for blind children. These children too are experiencing the deprivation of a maternal figure and loss of brothers, sisters, friends, and all the familiar elements that have given the world meaning. In addition, an unknown new situation is fraught with fears which further threaten a child's sense of security.

In such cases, adults are faced with a two-fold challenge; first, to ease the shock of disruption of maternal and environmental ties, and second, to provide the opportunity for a child to establish new ties and reassure himself that there are people who care about him as a person and who stand ready to further his emotional well-being. In practice one can ease the break from the familiarity of home and help assuage fear of a new institution by permitting a familiar person to accompany a child to the new place. In addition, a familiar toy, a beloved toy animal, or even a favourite blanket can reassure a child that all is not lost, and some vestiges of home life link him to the place and people he loves best. This plan is always possible in the case of a child coming from his own home for treatment in hospitals or therapy centres. Ideally a mother should accompany him and remain with him for a day or more, if necessary. Where a child is coming from a broken home, or if he has been abandoned, one must get along without the benefit of a familiar person in the new surroundings.

The second challenge can always be met. Every effort should be made to assign a particular staff member to look after each child so that there is someone whom he can trust and on whom he may depend. He seeks someone who is interested in him and in whom he may vest some of the feeling he had bestowed upon his mother. Furthermore, staff members should be trained to expect a child to regress and become more infantile than his age would warrant. Regression might take the form of clinging, or of withdrawing from social contacts or attempts to help himself. Defensive behaviour might be manifested as well, through hostility or unpredictable crying. It must be accepted as the expression of a child's distress, and the acceptance of it must be used to reaffirm his dependency on a staff person who cares about him. This means that staff members must be trained to anticipate such difficulties in the first few weeks after a child enters an institution and to accept them as part of the challenge of their work.

Such considerations about the mental health of children in institutions are particularly pertinent to centres which offer physical treatment. In many cases, the direct appeal of a child who has an obvious physical defect which cripples him and sets him aside from the normal activity of childhood has resulted in a strong emotional response from communities which supply large sums of money for beautiful buildings with the latest equipment for exercise and the correction of abnormalities. Such places are administered by people who are especially adept in treatment of physical disabilities, which is their main concern. Being competent and successful people themselves, they are sometimes blind to the emotional needs of the children who come under their care, and the tendency is to ignore the human aspect of care which might contribute to mental health.

We now know that physical health can be promoted by a period of time in hospital while mental health is being undermined at the same time. Our communities now have adequate knowledge and resources to promote physical and emotional well-being coincidently. The need remains for specialists in each area to integrate their knowledge and to educate the public to the importance of both. Each year brings new knowledge about developmental deficiencies and deviations and their treatment. With the knowledge comes the need for constant vigilance on the part of administrators of children's institutions to keep abreast of new developments, evaluate their efficacy, and integrate them appropriately into their programmes to provide optimal recovery for the children in their care. Had the staff of the Neil McNeil Home had available the knowledge about the retraining of a neurological organization, as propounded by Delacato at a later date (16), the degree of recovery might have been advanced beyond the level we were able to achieve at the time.

Research findings on the results of maternal deprivation inevitably will reflect differences for years to come, because the problems are complex and relatively little knowledge can be achieved at one time. Only as knowledge is accumulated from a variety of studies can any meaningful integration of conclusions take place. One of the most fruitful methods of study is the longitudinal one, whereby children can be observed closely for a long period of time and the course of their lives studied. Although sometimes lacking the incisiveness of more scientifically designed studies, it nevertheless provides information about the effectiveness of people living in a milieu of human relationships and cultural values. Such an investigation of the children from the Neil McNeil Home is still in progress, and reports on them will continue to be published through their adolescence. The method has already proven its worth in this study, where the children's remarkable recovery from a deprived state has been carefully documented and demonstrated.

APPENDICES

Infant Security Scale

DIRECTIONS FOR THE INFANT SECURITY SCALE

Our present understanding of children's development leads us to believe that healthy children show a mixture of behaviour, some of which is pleasing to and approved by adults, and some of which is disturbing and difficult. We believe that each child has his unique combination of easy and difficult behaviour, and that this pattern will change from time to time as he grows older. New environmental demands will create new patterns of behaviour. At times he will seem more in harmony with his world than at others.

The attached rating form includes statements that refer to both kinds of behaviour. They are intended to describe the child as he has been "generally" in the past few weeks. It is expected that many infants will show some of the kinds of behaviour described in all three columns.

In selecting the items which apply to a child, your judgment will be most accurate if you do not hesitate long in your decisions.

Directions for Endorsing the Items

1. Place a check ($\checkmark$) to the right, beside the item which generally describes the child's behaviour as he is now and has been recently.

2. If you find yourself debating a choice of items in two or three columns, check each one. Children are often inconsistent at this age and show contradictory behaviour rather than consistency.

3. Where there are detailed descriptive terms listed under a general item (e.g., cries, whines, frets), would you underline the particular ones which apply, or make an addition.

4. Check as many times as you wish. The unchecked items will be those which you feel do not apply.

5. Because of the rapid changes in development during the period of infancy, some of the items will not apply, either because they have not yet become a part of the child's experience, or because he has grown through the stage when a particular kind of behaviour is expected. Such an item is, "Takes to spoon feeding readily," which does not apply after spoon feeding has been established. When this arises with the child you are describing, mark "O" (omit).

Example of Checking

Protests when new foods offered ✔
- — <u>Pushes hand</u>
- — <u>Spits out</u>
- — Cries
- — Fusses

Please ignore the asterisks. They refer only to groups of items for research analysis.

INFANT SECURITY SCALE

C.A.: 7.8 months
Age: 0–24 Months
Date: Feb. 21, 1958   Birth date June 28, 1957
Name: 4   Admitted July 12, 1957

EATING					
Takes to spoon feeding readily	✓	Unhappy at mealtime		Refuses spoon feeding	
*Accepts new foods readily	✓			Protests when new foods offered —turns away —pushes hand —spits out —cries —fusses	
Enthusiastic about food —bottle —solids	✓	Poor eater		Objects at feeding time —cries —frets —doesn't finish	
*Accepts opportunity to try to feed self —cup —spoon	O	Resents having to feed self	O	Refuses to feed self when expected to do so	O
Waits patiently when reassured the meal is coming		Resents waiting for meals	✓	Impatient despite reassurances that meal is coming —whines —cries	✓
Permits self to be fed when necessary	✓	Resents being fed		Gets angry if not allowed to feed himself	
*Co-operates when unfamiliar person is in charge at meal time —sitter —visitor	✓	Apprehensive unless a familiar person is around at meal time		Refuses to eat unless familiar person is in charge at meal time —sitter —visitor	
Unconcerned if tray is mussy	✓	Upset by mussy tray		Refuses to eat if tray is mussy	

INFANT SECURITY SCALE—Continued

SLEEPING					
*Sleeps readily in new bed or new surroundings	√	Resistant attitude towards sleep		Cries when placed in unfamiliar bed or unfamiliar surroundings	
Accepts bed without protest	√			Protests when put to bed —cries —fusses	
*Adjusts easily to a new position for sleep		Poor sleeper		Content only in a familiar position for sleep	√
Sound sleeper Relaxed in sleep	√			Fitful sleeper Light sleeper Restless sleeper —cries out —twitches —jumps —turns	
*Accepts being put to bed by anyone	√	Apprehensive unless familiar person is around at bed time		Protests when put to bed by unfamiliar person —cries —fumes —stands up	
TOILET					
Accepts or co-operates when changed —diaper —panties —sleepers	√	Unhappy when diaper changed —uncomfortable —angry	O	Refuses to co-operate when being changed —cries —kicks —rolls over —hits —pinches	√
Accepts being placed on potty or toidy	O	Fearful of toidy	O	Cries when placed on potty or toidy	O
Relaxed when having bowel movement	√	Loose stools or constipation		Cries when having bowel movement	
Indicates need for toilet or dry clothing by —pointing —clutching self —grunting	O	Anxious about toilet training	O	Concerned about toilet needs —must be changed at once —constantly demands to go —wakens crying for toilet	O

INFANT SECURITY SCALE—Continued

BATH				
Enjoys bath	✓	Fearful of bath	Cries or becomes tense when bathed	
Accepts having ears and nose cleaned			Resists having ears and nose cleaned	✓
*Relaxed when bathed, washed, or toileted by unfamiliar person	✓	Apprehensive unless familiar person present at bath, wash, and toilet	Tense and uncertain when bathed, washed, or toileted by unfamiliar person —visitor —baby sitter	
PHILOSOPHY				
Enjoys rough play —bouncing —dandling —tossing —pushing	✓	Seems fearful physically	Cries or becomes tense when played with roughly —bouncing —dandling —tossing —pushing	
Recovers readily from hurts —physical —feelings	✓	Unresponsive to physical affection	Sulks or cries long after being comforted.	
Enjoys cuddling	✓		Dislikes cuddling —squirms —restless —pushes away	
*Enjoys change of environment —outside in carriage —shopping —visiting	✓	Fearful of change of environment	Withdraws or cries when environment changed —outside in carriage —shopping —visiting	
Enjoys unusual appearance of familiar figure —hair curlers —scarf on hair —dark glasses	✓		Cries or withdraws from unusual appearance of familiar figure —hair curlers —scarf on hair —dark glasses	
Enjoys physical activity —kicking —rolling over —bouncing —crawling —climbing	✓	Physically apathetic and listless	Little spontaneous physical activity	
Amuses self happily in fairly restricted play area	✓	Very sensitive to physical sensations	Cries or whines when in restricted play area	

INFANT SECURITY SCALE   Continued

PHILOSOPHY —Continued				
Accepts interference to physical activity —being picked up —being dressed	✓		Cries, kicks, whines when physical activity is interfered with —being picked up —being dressed	✓
Amuses self with vocal play	✓		Rarely vocalizes	
Enjoys car rides	O		Cries or becomes ill when riding in cars	O
Enjoys a crowd	O	Frightened in a crowd	O	Cries, turns to mother in a crowd	O
Unconcerned if mussy or dirty	✓		Insists on being clean and tidy	
			Frequently sucks thumb or fingers	✓
			Rocks, pulls own hair, pulls ears.	
			Frequent temper tantrums	
SOCIAL				
Content when left to play alone	✓	Unusual sensitivity to the presence of others		Cries or whines when left to play alone	
Enjoys the presence of people other than the family	O		Frets or turns to mother in the presence of others	O
Can respond to sudden advances from a stranger	✓		Cries at the sudden advances of a stranger	
Enjoys the company of other children	✓		Uncomfortable in the company of other children	
Can accept shared attention	✓		Cries or pushes other children when they receive attention	
Enjoys being left alone with other children	✓		Cries or whines when left alone with other children	
Enjoys unusual tone of voice —noisy —rough			Cries or whines at unusual tone of voice —noisy —rough	

INFANT SECURITY SCALE—Continued

PHILOSOPHY —Continued					
Accepts being left alone with strangers —neighbour —baby sitter	O			Cries when left alone with strangers —neighbour —baby sitter	O
Stands up for himself	√			Lets other children bully him —take his toys	
Likes to "converse" with others —chattering	√	Seems shy, apathetic in presence of others		Clams up when spoken to Indifferent in presence of others	√
PLAY					
Watches toys within vision	√	Lacks interest in play material		Ignores toys within vision	
Clutches toys and hangs on	√			Drops toys when placed in his hand	
Manipulates play material —mouths —examines —bangs —explores possibilities —enjoys noise	√			Restricted manipulation of play materials —seldom mouths —seldom examines —seldom bangs —listless use —little variety in use	
Reaches for play material enthusiastically	√			Quickly loses interest in play materials	
Doesn't mind giving up toys —to parents —to children	√	Feelings hurt when toys taken away		Clings to own toys	
*Eager for new toys	√	Fearful of new toys		Withdraws from or ignores new toys	√

Pre-school Mental Health Assessment Scale

Pre-school Record

All the items of behaviour on this record have been shown by healthy pre-school children. The child of whom you are thinking will have his own unique assortment. He, of course, changes constantly as he grows and learns and as circumstances alter. Sometimes he will respond easily to one aspect of life, sometimes to another as he develops. To have difficulties is a part of healthy development.

This record is to obtain a portrayal of his particular pattern of response during the present period.

In selecting the items which apply to a child your judgment will be most accurate if you do not hesitate long in your decisions.

Directions for Checking Items

Place a check (✔) to the left beside each item which generally describes the child's behaviour as he (she) is now and has been in the near past.

If you find yourself debating on choice of items in the two columns, check in both columns. Children are inconsistent at this age and show a variety of behaviour rather than sameness.

Where there are details listed under an item, encircle the particular description which applied to the child, or make an addition.

Check as many items as you wish. The unchecked items will be those that you feel do not apply.

In some cases a general statement will not be applicable because the situation does not arise with the child and has not become a part of his experience. In this case, mark "O" (omit). For example:

Can the child be left with adults other than parents? Mark "O" when the child has never been left without his parents.

Example of Checking

✔ Disturbing at mealtime
— dawdles, plays, over-talkative, restless, getting up

Please ignore the asterisks. They refer only to the grouping of items for research purposes.

Add any comments, criticisms, or descriptive remarks you wish in the right-hand column.

Prepared by D. A. Millichamp
January, 1956

INSTITUTE OF CHILD STUDY

UNIVERSITY OF TORONTO

Home Report

NAME:..................... AGE:........ DATE:........... DONE BY: *Staff*

	X items		*Y items*	*Comments*
1	Enjoys being among other children	1	Withdrawn from other children	
2	Can get along in play with other children	2	Shows emotion in presence of other children —irritable, protests, cries, excited, hits out, grabs at, bites, impatient, cross, unpleasant	
3	Can maintain own rights with other children	3	Usually gives in to other children in play, routine, conversation	
4	Will accept that other child has rights in play	4	Often aggressive toward other children —teases, interferes with, takes toys, orders about, insists on own way	
5	Plays readily with any child of suitable age	5	Will play with one or two children of own choice only	
6	Enjoys being with sibling(s) Age(s): Sex:	6	Emotionally disturbed when sibling around —irritable, protesting, crying, excited, hits, grabs at, bites, impatient, cross, unpleasant	
7	Can maintain own rights with sibling(s)	7	Usually gives in to sibling(s)	
8	Will accept that sibling(s) has (have) rights	8	Usually agressive toward sibling(s) —teases, interferes with, takes things away from, bosses	
9	Can accept shared adult attention with sibling(s)	9	Disturbed by parent attention to sibling(s) —plays for attention to self —withdraws —shows emotion: protests, whines, cries, temper tantrums, excited, hits, pushes adult or child	
		10	Overly-attached and attentive to sibling(s) —follows around —tries to do as sibling does —repeated demonstrations of affection	
		11	Apathetic toward other children	

	X items		Y items	Comments
10	Venturesome physically	12	Avoids venturesome play —shows emotion: runs away, protests, cries	
11	Recovers readily by himself from hurt	13	Undue show of emotion when hurt —frequent, prolonged, cries, sulks, screams	
12	Can be reassured when hurt	14	a. Refuses to be reassured by adult b. Seeks adult reassurance for all hurts c. Shows excessive emotion when treated for minor hurts —running away, violent struggling, screaming	
13	Enjoys car rides	15	Is upset by car rides —screams, ill	
14	Interested in seeing trains, aeroplanes, animals	16	Shows emotion when sees train, aeroplane, animal —runs away, tearful, clings, cries, temper tantrums	
15	Usually accepts preparation to go to Nursery School in matter-of-fact way	17	Emotionally upset about going to Nursery School —refuses, cries, sulks, temper tantrums, clings	
16	Accepts unusual figure, e.g., clown, Santa Claus	18	Emotionally upset by unusual figures —runs away, tearful, clings, cries, temper tantrums	
		19	Has habitual tic—thumb-sucking, finger-sucking, masturbation appearing —during sleep, routines, play —when tired, upset, waiting	
		20	Is unduly attached to some object or article	
		21	Insists on performing certain set acts or rituals although unnecessary and diverting (e.g., opening and closing doors, etc.)	
17	Enjoys strenuous physical play	22	Frequent aimless activity at playtimes —outdoors —indoors	
18	Can amuse self happily for reasonable length of time with playthings	23	Settles to play only when given attention continually	
19	Content to play alone routinely —outdoors —indoors	24	Refuses to play alone —shows emotion: protesting, crying, temper tantrums, sulking	
20	Is interested in a variety of play activities and materials	25	Plays repeatedly with same material in same way	

	X items		Y items	Comments
21	Can concentrate on one play activity for a short period	26	Attention too readily diverted from a play activity	
22	Will accept substitute plaything or activity	27	Shows emotion when unable to have chosen plaything —protests, cries, whines, sulks, temper tantrums	
23	Accepts restrictions of play area, activity, and materials	28	Generally refuses to accept play restrictions —ignores, disobeys, argues, —shows emotion, protests, cries, temper tantrums, sulks	
		29	Frequently shows emotion when in difficulty with play materials —impatient, irritable, cries, sulks, temper tantrums	
		30	Apathetic toward play —outdoors —indoors	
24	Responds readily to physical demonstrations of affection —by father —by mother	31	Tends to withdraw from parent demonstrations of affection —from father —from mother —shows emotion: shrinks from, stiffens, —protests, cries, sulks, temper tantrums, hits	
25	Seeks physical comfort —from father —from mother	32	Often refuses care and help —from father —from mother —shows emotion: irritable, cross, protests, struggles, cries, temper tantrums, sulks, argues, hits	
26	Generally accepts care and help —from father —from mother			
27	Generally accepts direction —by father —by mother	33	Often negative to direction —from father —from mother —shows emotion: refuses, ignores, argues, rude, irritable, cross, protests, struggles, cries, temper tantrums, sulks, hits —when corrected or criticized by parent, shows emotion, tearful, cries, sulks, unhappy, arguing	
28	Enjoys being in the company of adults	34	Shows emotion in the presence of unfamiliar adults —subdued, runs away, holds onto parents, cries, excited	

	X items		Y items	Comments
29	Can accept being left with adults other than parents	35	Remains emotionally upset when left with an adult other than parents —refuses to respond, runs away, cries, temper tantrums, sulks	
30	Can amuse self when parents or adults are otherwise occupied	36	Continually interrupts parent and adults with demands for attention	
31	Enjoys being in a crowd	37	Shows emotion in a crowd —clings, cries, excited	
		38	Over-conforms —adheres to all adult expectation —refers unnecessarily for adult direction	
32	Shows an interest in dressing and un-dressing	39	Refuses to get dressed and undressed —fusses, postpones, argues	
		40	Emotionally upset about dressing —protesting, impatient, whining, crying, temper tantrums, pulling away, excited	
33	Takes part when capable in dressing	41	Waits or asks for unnecessary help in dressing	
34	Accepts necessary help in dressing	42	Refuses to allow adult to assist dress	
35	Co-operates in following expected dressing routine	43	Inattentive to dressing —dawdles, plays, over-talkative, careless	
		44	Overly interested in clothes and appearance —overly conscious of clothes —overly careful of clothing	
		45	Emotionally upset over clothing —if clothes get dirty or torn or mussed —insists on choosing and wearing particular things —if not allowed, protests, whines, cries, temper tantrums	
		46	General lack of effort or concern toward dressing	
36	Matter-of-fact acceptance of toileting —bowels —bladder	47	Frequently refuses to try at toilet when taken —argues	
		48	Emotionally upset when taken to toilet —protests, whines, cries, excited, impatient	

	X items		Y items	Comments
		49	Physical retention at toilet, postpones going to toilet	
37	Can function readily at toilet —bowels —bladder	50	Has difficulty functioning physically at toilet —bowels —bladder	
38	Looks after self with help	51	Demands or waits for unnecessary assistance at toilet	
39	Accepts accidents but indicates need to be clean	52	Emotionally upset when wet or soiled —whining, crying, excited —tries to hide fact when wet or soiled —refuses to be changed when wet or soiled —pays no attention when wet or soiled	
40	Recognizes need to go to toilet in waking hours	53	Shows very little control of elimination —frequently wet and does not go to toilet —frequently soiled and does not go at toilet	
41	Accepts unfamiliar toilet arrangements, unfamiliar surroundings, unfamiliar persons present	54	Disturbed by unfamiliar toilet arrangements, surroundings, persons —does not go to toilet —refuses to go —emotionally upset	
42	Co-operative in going to toilet as expected	55	Inattentive at toilet —dawdling, playing, over-talkative, careless	
		56	Goes to toilet over-frequently —constantly demands —frequently takes self —wakes crying for toilet	
		57	Irregular eliminative functioning	
		58	General lack of effort or concern about elimination and toileting	
		59	Overinterested in function —deliberate wetting or soiling —plays with urine, faeces —overly attentive to others' functioning	
		60	Recurring interest in body parts Overly curious about others' genitals —frequent handling of own genitals —masturbates —recurring sex play with children —exhibits body parts	

	X items		Y items	Comments
43	Enjoys eating	61	Shows lack of any interest in food —slow, dawdling, picks at food	
44	Likes most foods	62	Often shows dislike —definite dislike of certain foods —erratic in likes and dislikes	
45	Amount eaten at meal-time is fairly consistent	63	Eats erratically; either a lot or a little —eats between rather than at mealtimes	
46	Expects to feed self except in special circumstances	64	Prefers to be fed —refuses to feed self	
47	Is co-operative in carrying out expected meal-time precedure	65	Disturbing at mealtime —dawdles, plays, over-talkative, restless, getting up	
48	Usually waits pleasantly for meals	66	Shows emotion when waiting for food —impatient, whines, cries, temper tantrums	
49	Will eat with anyone in charge	67	Does not eat as usual if not supervised by usual person —emotionally upset, refusing, crying, temper tantrums, sulking	
50	Attempts new foods readily	68	Refuses new foods —emotionally upset, complains, whines, cries, temper tantrums	
		69	Intense refusal of food shown by —regurgitating, spitting out, holding in mouth, gagging —refusing to taste	
51	Seems content to be settled into bed	70	Struggles against lying down and resting —very restless, gets out, asks for toys	
52	Relaxes and lies quietly when settled in bed	71	Shows emotion when put in bed —protests, whines, cries, temper tantrums, excited	
53	Sound sleeper	72	Disturbed in sleep —physically restless, cries out, wakens crying, frequent nightmares, night walking	
54	Relaxed sleeper			

	X items		Y items	Comments
55	Rests comfortably until goes to sleep	73	Remains awake restless for long periods —calling, getting out, playing	
56	Co-operative in bedtime procedure (getting ready, etc.)	74	Objects regularly at bedtime —dawdles, plays, runs away, shows emotion: refusing, whining, crying, temper tantrums	
57	Goes off to sleep as usual when arrangement is unfamiliar —unfamiliar surroundings, put to bed by unfamiliar person, bedtime altered	75	Does not sleep as usual if arrangements unfamiliar —strange surroundings, strange person, routine altered	
		76	Poor sleeper	
		77	Frequent wakes in morning —cross, irritable, crying, refusing, temper tantrums	
58	Wakes up ready to get up, cheerful	78	Has special fixed bedtime ritual —special thing, toy, blanket —special acts, —recurring tic: e.g., sucking blanket —shows emotion if not followed: refusing, crying, temper tantrums	
		79	Disturbed by darkness —asks for light, sleeps with light —shows emotion (whimpers, cries, temper tantrums) if left in dark	
		80	Tired and sleepy but does not go to sleep	
		81	Seems overly tired most of the time	

Staff Records and Instructions

Samples of staff bulletins and record form used for staff training and reports of observations of the children

These children are in this Institution for many reasons, but the only one we are interested in is that they depend on us to care about them.

When you are with a child, try to think of him not just as a baby, but as a little person with *feelings*. He needs your love and guidance, even if it is only a few hours a week. Everything you do for him will help him grow and develop in all areas of his life.

A FEW RULES

1. Please phone if for any reason you cannot come on duty. It is the children who will suffer if their grown-up friend does not turn up.

2. Always remember to sign on duty because that is the way we keep the pay sheet up to date. (You are paid every two weeks on a Monday.) Your Supervisor will show you the notice board with your name on the list.

3. Your time on duty and days off will also be on this notice board.

4. *How to dress.*
    (a) A plain smock that covers you completely, in a pretty colour such as green, blue, or red. However, we would prefer you to wear a washable nylon uniform in a plain colour. Two of these will be sufficient. These wash and dry very quickly and require no ironing.
    (b) Low walking shoes.
    (c) Short, tidy hair. If you have long hair, please do it up and wear a hair net if necessary.
    (d) Moderate make-up.

5. Before you go to the nurseries or handle the children will you please remember to *wash your hands*.

6. This is a rehabilitation period for these institution children. Plans and the system of doing things will be changed often, so be prepared for

anything. Supervisors will not be far away and are there to help you. Don't be afraid to ask *why we do things and why the children behave as they do.*

7. Ask for a list of your duties. Write them down, if it is confusing. Look carefully at the schedules posted for children and staff. Familiarize yourself with these schedules but remember—as the children are ready and can accept a new programme, schedules will be changed.

8. You are expected to bring your own lunch and eat it in the staff living room. Meals are not provided due to the fact that the kitchen is being reorganized to provide the type of meals the children require.

SOME SUGGESTIONS TO FOLLOW

While these children are developing and growing, they are *learning.* If they have learned to trust grown-ups because adults do *care,* they will want to respond to them and the world about them. They will then grow according to their ability:

1. Spiritually;
2. Emotionally (this means attitudes and feelings—learning to be happy—controlling temper tantrums and fears);
3. Socially (this means learning to get along with other people—children and adults);
4. Physically;
5. Mentally.

You can help children do this when you are with them:

1. *When you are changing a baby's diaper*
   (*a*) Never leave him alone on the dressing table—or in bed with the side down.
   (*b*) Talk to him quietly, smile at him, use simple words; this helps him to babble and learn to talk. He will try to talk to you if he knows you want to talk to him. Sing to him and see what happens.
   (*c*) See that he is very clean, washed, powdered, and comfortable before you put his panties on. *Watch for any rashes* or anything you are in doubt about and *report immediately* to the nurse.

2. *When you are feeding him*
   (*a*) Cuddle him when you are giving him his bottle. Talk to him quietly, smile at him, use simple words; this helps him to babble and learn to talk. He will try to talk to you if he knows you want to talk to him.
   (*b*) If you are helping to feed him, don't hurry him—don't force him to eat. We want him to *learn* to enjoy food. Remember we don't all eat the same amount.
   If the baby is learning to feed himself by getting his fingers in his dinner, don't be annoyed, just put the spoon in his hand. It may be months before he is really feeding himself but that is a start. Remember, you are helping him to learn the right way. He is going

to learn anyway, but a child can learn the wrong way *if we do not help him*.

3. *When you are bathing him*
   (*a*) Never leave him alone on the table. Talk to him quietly, smile at him, use simple words.
   (*b*) If he is fearful of a bath, give him a sponge bath. If you can help it, *don't cause a crying spell* because a child is afraid. (If you are confused about difference between screaming through fear and having a temper tantrum because of anger, please talk to your Child Development Supervisor. You want the child to learn to trust you and enjoy a bath.)
   (*c*) If he does enjoy his bath,
       (*1*) watch the temperature—test water with your elbow;
       (*2*) play with him in his bath. Make bath time a happy time. This is one time he has you all to *himself*.

4. *Playtime*. All children *learn* while playing. Except for eating, sleeping, toileting, and bathing, a little child's waking hours are spent experimenting with the things around him. It may be an iron bed post, an electric light switch, a rocking horse, dishes, dolls, or blocks.
   Try to remember to give a little child a toy he can experiment with and do something with that will develop *thinking*. In other words, help him to use his mind. For example, help him to put one block on top of another and then let him try it himself. Pat and cuddle a doll and see if he will try to imitate you. Show him how to do things, *but don't make him*. He will learn to do it *his way*, not *yours*.
   There are many things in a little child's life he has to learn *our way*.
   (*a*) He cannot hit people.
   (*b*) He cannot destroy other people's belongings.
   (*c*) He cannot run on the road when he does not understand the danger.
   (*d*) He must go to bed when we want him to.
   But, when he is playing he should be free to *learn* at his own pace. Remember we can help him by giving him the right kind of toys and equipment to play with.
   These children in Neil McNeil need a great deal of individual help. They are institution babies and have been deprived of the most important thing in their lives—*parents* and people who *care*. All of us can help fill this gap.
   Help the child to trust you.
   Give him a feeling of inner comfort by approving of him as a real person. (He is going to make mistakes in this business of learning to grow up—but haven't we all.)
   When you have been at Neil McNeil a few weeks, we will talk more about these *children's needs, their behaviour problems* and what we mean by *learning—feelings—discipline*.

M. Kilgour
February 11, 1958   *Pre-school Consultant*

STAFF REPORT ON CHILDREN

NAME OF CHILD _____BIRTH DATE _____

HOUSE MOTHER _____TELEPHONE NO. _____

When you have completed this form, will you please discuss it with the Child Development Supervisor.

How long have you worked with child: _____

How long has the child been in present unit? _____

Date of transfer to unit _____

Underline the behaviour that appears applicable to you.

1. (*a*) With other children, is the child—indifferent—interested—
     co-operative? _____

   _____

   (*b*) Do other children worry him, frustrate him, or does he really enjoy
     them? _____

   (*c*) Is he aggressive if another child interferes in what he wants to do?

   _____

   _____

   (*d*) Have you seen the child with children of his own age or older
     (other than his own institution companions)? If so describe the
     circumstances. _____

   _____

   _____

   _____

   _____

2. (*a*) Does the child accept you alone—respond to you—seek your
     relationship? _____

   _____

   _____

   (*b*) Is child interested only in what you are doing with him?—is he
     indifferent towards you, does he enjoy you as a trusted friend?

   _____

   _____

   _____

(c) Has he shown signs of being very demanding of your attention? If so, describe briefly. _____

_____

_____

_____

_____

_____

3. (a) When the child is using play materials such as books, puzzles, small toys, is he destructive—lacking of purpose—constructive? _____

_____

_____

(b) When using equipment, does he appear apathetic—anxious—enthusiastic? _____

_____

_____

(c) Can child stay at one activity for any length of time (enquire Child Development Supervisor)? _____
Does his concentration span appear short, fair, very good? _____

_____

_____

(d) Does he require your help to be attentive? _____

_____

(e) Does his activity outdoors appear aimless—venturesome—purposeful? _____

_____

_____

4. Describe any new situations that the child has encountered with you that have made him fearful and anxious. _____

_____

_____

_____

_____

5. (a) Describe specific situations that have given rise to temper tantrums
       in past month. _____

   _____

   _____

   _____

   _____

   _____

   (b) Does he accept routines such as
       (1) toileting,
       (2) going to bed,
       (3) bathing and washing,
       (4) dressing and undressing,
       (5) going to and from nursery school or playground,
       (6) eating?

   _____

   _____

   (c) Describe any of these procedures child is having difficulty with.

   _____

   _____

   _____

   _____

   _____

   _____

   (d) Did the child refuse discipline and direction? Do you feel he will
       accept discipline from you? _____

   _____

   _____

   _____

6. Describe any habits or tics that you have observed, such as thumb-
   sucking, rocking, blinking, stuttering, masturbating, etc. _____

   _____

   _____

   _____

7. (a) observe speech of the child. Is he babbling, attempting words by repeating after you, using sentences? _____

_____

_____

(b) If child can converse, have you seen signs of imaginative play (pretending)? Describe. _____

_____

_____

_____

_____

8. Describe briefly any experiences you have given child to enrich his life, i.e. walk in park, visits to church, stores, zoo, your home, rides in car, boats, etc. How has he responded? _____

_____

_____

_____

_____

_____

_____

_____

9. Is child receiving individual help in a controlled setting—attending Neil McNeil Nursery School or a nursery school in the community?

_____

_____

_____

Volunteer Records and Instructions

Following are samples of information distributed to volunteers, record forms with directions regarding observations which were used to train volunteers, and finally, a form to be completed by a volunteer once she was well acquainted with her child. The latter report was used by the staff to supplement their knowledge of a child when he was beyond the confines of his institutional home.

TO THOSE WHO ARE HELPING CHILDREN FOR A FEW HOURS—VOLUNTEERS

These children at this time are in this Institution for many reasons, but the only one we are interested in is that they depend on us to *care* about them.

When you are with a child, try to think of him not just as a baby, but as a little person with *feelings*. He needs your love and guidance, even if it is only for a few hours a week. Everything you do for him will help him grow and develop in all areas of his life.

A FEW THINGS TO REMEMBER WHEN YOU COME TO NEIL MCNEIL

1. Please phone if you cannot for any reason report when you said you would.
2. If you are a *volunteer*, we would appreciate if you would report to Child Development Office, pick up your yellow smock, and make enquiries about your specific child or children.

   If you are not happy in the type of help you have promised to do at Neil McNeil, there is a place for you somewhere else. *Do let us know.*
3. Before you go to the nurseries or handle the children, will you please remember to (*a*) wash your hands, (*b*) wear your smock, and be prepared for anything. Supervisors will not be far away and are there to help you help the children at all times.

   DON'T BE AFRAID TO ASK WHY WE DO THINGS AND WHY THE CHILDREN BEHAVE AS THEY DO
4. Ask for a list of your duties. Write them down if it is confusing. Look carefully at the schedules posted for children. Familiarize yourself with these schedules.

VOLUNTEER SERVICE

First Observation Day

If you are a daytime Volunteer—
1. Go to the Nursery School, second floor, and, weather permitting, leave your coat and get your smock.
2. Always *wash your hands* before going into the Nursery or Playroom. Try to make this a routine habit after coming in off the street.
3. Look at the notice board for messages if the Volunteer Supervisor is not there.
4. Proceed to the Main House and enquire in the Child Development Office where you are to go.
5. Mark the time of your arrival in the red Volunteer Record Book on the table in the vestibule. When you leave also mark the time of your departure.
6. Proceed to Unit, Playroom, or Garden for observation.
   (a) Sit quietly in a low chair (so that you will be on the same level as the children) and WATCH.
   (b) Watch the adults and the responses of the children. Look at
       What the children play with,
       How long they play with it, and
       How they use it.
   Are the children playing with other children or running about by themselves when they are in the garden?
   Have a small notebook in which to jot down your observations and any questions which you might like to discuss with the Volunteer Supervisor.

Second Observation Day

1. Go to Nursery School, second floor. Leave your coat, get your smock and wash your hands.
2. Look on the Notice Boards in the Nursery School and the vestibule of Neil McNeil for any messages or suggestions.
3. Have you remembered to mark the red Volunteer Record Book? Have you seen a Volunteer Supervisor or Child Development Supervisor? We do want you to begin to feel at home.
4. Proceed to Unit, Playroom, or Garden (not the same one as last week) for another day of observation.
   Sit quietly and just watch. When you are with the children never stand when you can sit, so that they will not have to look up to you. This creates a quieting atmosphere. They have been used to adults and children rushing about and noises becoming louder and louder. Every effort to quiet these children is a step in the right direction.
   Have you noticed their behaviour and their habits in a large group?
   What are they like when they are alone with an adult?
   Have you noticed any difference in the behaviour and personalities of the little children in comparison with the older children? The younger children are developing in a more normal way because they have not

been deprived as long—deprived of toys, play, opportunities for learning, being *loved* and *loving* in return.

Third Observation Day

1. Have you remembered to get your smock, wash your hands, and mark the time of your arrival in the Volunteer Record Book?
2. Have you looked on the Notice Boards for anything new in the way of suggestions? Have *you* any suggestions to leave us?
3. Would you like to join the Neil McNeil Auxiliary? As a member you would be part of a large group whose goal is to help our institutional children to have as normal a life as possible, if they cannot live in their own or substitute (Foster and Adopting) homes. The President of the Auxiliary is . . . .
4. Have you had a Chest X-Ray within the last year? Since you will be in such close contact with the children, we feel that this is a necessary precautionary measure.
5. There are many ways in which a Volunteer may help—sewing, knitting, painting and mending toys, driving children to the clinic, *or* being a special friend to a child.
   If you feel that you are ready to have a child to whom you will give special attention, go to the Child Development Supervisor and ask her which child needs the most help. Remember that some of these little children have hidden worries or are too aggressive and demanding. Most of them have problems which they have not yet learned to solve. You will be helping a little one to gain trust in adults so that, when the time comes, he can relate to other people more easily. When you have to give him up for adoption, a foster home, or any other reason, you will have the consolation of knowing that you have given something of yourself to him and have helped him on his road to maturity.
6. The children are in different Units. When you have been assigned to a Unit, look at the children's schedule carefully. Unless you have been assigned to a specific job in the Unit, ask the Unit Mother or Supervisor to have the child brought to you. This will be less confusing to you and to the Staff and will ensure that the programme in the Unit is not interrupted.

Suggested Programme for You and Child—2 Hours

— Take child off by himself. Ground-floor children to basement playroom or Nursery School playroom. Second-floor children to Yellow Room or Infirmary playroom.
— Try to do something quiet and gentle with the child, do not stimulate him. He is living in an "electric atmosphere" most of the time. Speak to him quietly.
— Give him a changing experience by taking him for a walk in a carriage (sign out at the office when you do this).
— Look at picture books.
— Let him play in a basin of water or sail a boat in the bath tub.
— Listen to records.
— Play quietly with toys at a table.

— Do not play boisterously with these children, as that is their pattern of behaviour most of the time.
— When you have finished with your child, take his hand and bring him back to his Unit Mother. Remember that a handclasp is a sign of trust between two friends.
— When you are ready to leave, mark the time of your departure in the Volunteer Record Book.

INSTRUCTIONS TO VOLUNTEERS

From: MISS KILGOUR, *Supervisor*

a. If you wish to bring your children any little toys, perhaps you could obtain a nylon bag from Woolworths to put them in. They would be kept in his cupboard on his hook to use when you are with him.
b. If you are a knitter, a little plain hat or bonnet of his very own would be appreciated. It will be soon too warm for winter helmets. They should be made in bright colours, or with a pattern.
c. Watch bulletin board upstairs for suggestions and articles to read.
d. If you are in the garden with one or two children, will you try to encourage them to play as long as possible with the equipment they are using. *For example*—if he is pulling a wagon and looks as if he has lost interest in pulling it, show him how to put blocks in it, leaves, etc., or to pull another child. Help him to *think* of what to do.
e. If children are fighting over toys, pick the child up and say: "We do not do this. You may not have this until Bobby is finished with it."
f. If a child has a temper tantrum, carry him away from the other children and try to quiet him. If you cannot manage, carry him to a Supervisor. Carrying these children is not spoiling them. They have never had close adult relationship, and we are these children's friends. If you carry them, it means you are not annoyed at what they are doing but you are *helping them* to learn they cannot stay in the group and behave as they are. Children have to learn they cannot get what they want by screaming.

RULES FOR GARDEN

a. Watch the children every minute.
b. Help them to find something to do:
    — Use kiddie car.
    — Play in sand. (If they throw sand, take them out of the sandbox immediately and say: "We do not throw sand. You will have to play with something else. If you remember not to throw, you can go back."
    — Pull wagons.
    — Climb jungle gym—help them if they need it, but stay beside them.
    — Build with large blocks.
    — Push doll carriages.
    — Use swings.
    — Sweep leaves.

c. If you see anything dangerous in garden, get there first and remove it before the children do.

d. Children must not play with sticks. You say: "We don't play with sticks Johnny—it might hurt someone."

e. If it is time for the child to go inside, warn him first. "It will soon be time to go inside. I will help you take your kiddie car back."

f. When it is time to go, take his hand, show him you mean what you say, and take him.

    If a little child does not understand what you say, he will learn by your attitudes—pick him up lovingly and take him indoors.

g. See specific rules regarding outdoor equipment on the Notice Board.

VOLUNTEER TOY LADIES

In the evenings children are tired but very excitable. They need to learn that they must remain quietly in bed and you will bring them a toy box or a book. Quiet play with simple toys helps them relax.

If children get out of bed, will you kindly but firmly remove toy from child and call night staff.

5.30   Wheel toy-carts into corridor but not opposite door where children will see toys.

5.40   Go to door of bedroom and ask day staff if they are ready for toy boxes. (Blinds must be ¾ down—children sitting in bed.)

5.50   If day staff is on till 7 o'clock, they may wish toys but will probably want to be alone with their own children. Do not go into that room unless a staff member asks you to.

6.00   Take toy box to child in bed. Make a suggestion or help him with it and tell him you will be back to help when other children have toys. If children get out of bed, remove toys and call staff.

6.30   Blinds down completely.

6.35   Send child to toilet and tell him he can play with toy for a minute when he returns. When all 5 children are toileted, remove toys.

6.40   Cookies.

6.50   Record players, back rub.

7.00   Room should be quiet but children allowed to talk.

NOTE: No water and no calling for toilet—this is an attempt to stay up longer.

TOY BOXES FOR CHILDREN IN BED

To be used for quiet play—preparing for sleep.

Try to help him with toy—use his imagination—talk softly—do not stimulate child.

Give each child a turn at having a little time with you.

If child is getting bored with toy box and is beginning to get restless, *then* give him another toy box, but not until he has helped you put toys back in box.

If children get restless with toys or get out of bed, it means they are too tired to manage. Remove all toys immediately, pull blinds down completely. Replace toys with book if child has not gone to toilet. (If room is too noisy and all children's behaviour is beginning to be disruptive, do not give book.)

NEIL McNEIL HOME
VOLUNTEER RECORD FORM

Volunteer _____Date _____
Tel. No. _____

When you have completed this Form please discuss it with the Child Development Supervisor or the Volunteer Supervisor.

Name of Child. _____ Age._____
Date you commenced working with child. _____
How often do you visit child? _____
If you miss your regular visit, do you come another day to make up for it?

_____

Underline the behaviour that is applicable.

1. (a) With other children is the child indifferent, interested, co-operative?

   _____

   (b) Do other children threaten him, frustrate him or does he really enjoy them? _____

   (c) Is he aggressive if another child interferes in what he wants to do?

   _____

   (d) Have you seen the child with children of his own age or with older children (other than his own institution companions). If so, briefly describe the circumstances. _____

   _____

   _____

   _____

2. (a) Does the child accept you alone, respond to you, seek your relationship? _____

   (b) Is he interested only in what *you* are doing with him, is he indifferent towards you, does he enjoy you as a trusted friend? _____

3. (a) When the child is using play materials such as books, puzzles, small toys, is he constructive, destructive, lacking in purpose? _____

   _____

   (b) When using equipment does he appear apathetic, worried, enthusiastic? _____

(c) Is his concentration span short, fair, very good? _____

(d) Does he require your help to be attentive? _____

_____

4. Describe your child's large muscle co-ordination:

   (a) Is he standing, crawling, walking, climbing, riding a tricycle?

   (b) Is he apathetic, energetic? _____

5.   Describe any new situations that the child has encountered with
       you that have made him fearful or anxious. _____

       _____

       _____

       _____

6. (a) Describe any situations that have given rise to temper tantrum.

       _____

       _____

       _____

       _____

   (b) Did the child refuse discipline or direction? Do you feel that he will
       accept discipline from you? _____

       _____

       _____

       _____

7.   Describe any habits or tics that you have observed, such as thumb-
       sucking, rocking, blinking, stuttering, masturbating, etc. _____

       _____

       _____

       _____

8.   Observe speech of the child. Is he babbling, attempting words by
       repeating after you, using sentences? _____

       _____

       _____

       _____

9.   Describe briefly the experiences you have given the child to enrich his life; i.o., walk in the park, visits to church, stores, zoo, your home, rides in cars, boats, etc. How has he responded? _____

_____

_____

_____

_____

_____

_____

_____

_____

_____

_____

_____

_____

_____

_____

Do you always inform the Supervisor or Unit Mother(dressed in dark blue) when you take a child out? Remember that he is an Institution child and may have many fears, hidden anxieties, or worries that block him from venturing into the outside world. He may also be very demanding and want far too much for his own good. Maybe all he is ready for is to sit on your lap. You are giving of yourself to this little one and helping him to grow and develop into a real personality. He is counting on you. You must also be prepared to give him up to Adopting parents who will give him a permanent home or to Foster parents who will provide a temporary home and give him more than we at Neil McNeil can give him.

Helpful reading material

"Child from One to Six." U.S. Government, Children's Bureau. Price 25c. Obtainable at Neil McNeil.

"How Children Play for Fun and Learning." Better Living Booklet, Nelson Publishing Co., Toronto.

Enquire at Pre-school Parent Centre, 983 Bay Street, for more reading material and helpful suggestions on pre-school children.

References

1. AINSWORTH, MARY D. "Reversible and Irreversible Effects of Maternal Deprivation on Intellectual Development." Child Welfare League of America, Inc. January, 1962.
2. —— "Patterns of Attachment Shown by the Infant in Interaction with his Mother." *Merrill-Palmer Quart.* X: 1 (1964).
3. —— "The Effects of Maternal Deprivation: A Review of Findings and Controversy in the Context of Research Strategy in Deprivation of Maternal Care; A Reassessment of its Effects." Geneva: World Health Organization, 1962. Public Health Papers, No. 14. With a comprehensive bibliography of the literature on maternal deprivation.
4. AINSWORTH & BOWLBY, J. "Research Strategy in the Study of Mother-Child Separation." *Courrier* IV (1954), 105–131.
5. AUSUBEL, DAVID P. "Ego-Development and the Learning Process." *Child Develpm.* XX (1947), 173–190.
6. BAKWIN, H. "Loneliness in Infants." *Amer. J. Dist. Child* LXIII (1942), 30.
7. —— "Emotional Deprivation in Infants." *J. Pedia.* XXXV (1949), 512.
8. BELLER, E. K. "Dependency and Independence in Young Children." *Amer. Psychologist* V (1950), 293.
9. BLATZ, W. E. "Understanding the Young Child." Toronto: Clarke Irwin, 1944.
10. BOWLBY, J. "The Influence of Early Environment in the Development of Neurosis and Neurotic Character." *Int. J. Psycho-Anal.* XXI (1940), 154.
11. ——"Maternal Care and Mental Health." Geneva: World Health Organization, 1952. Monograph Series, No. 2.
12. BOWLBY; AINSWORTH, M.; BOSTON, M.; and ROSENBLUTH, D. "The Effects of Mother-Child Separation: A Follow-up Study." *Brit. J. med. Psychol.* XXIX (1956), 211.
13. CALDWELL, BETTYE. "The Effects of Infant Care." *Child Development Review.* Hoffman & Hoffman, ed. Philadelphia: Wm. F. Fell & Co., 1963.
14. CLARKE, A. D. B. & CLARKE, A. M. "Recovery from the Effects of Deprivation." *Acta Psychol. Amst.* XVI (1959), 137.

15. ———— "Some Recent Advances in the Study of Early Deprivation." *J. Child Psychol. Psychiat.* I (1960), 26.

10. DELACATO, CARL H. *The Treatment and Prevention of Reading Problems.* Toronto: Ryerson Press, 1959.

17. ESCALONA, S.; LEITCH, M.; et. al. "Early Phases of Personality Development: A Normative Study of Infant Behaviour." Monograph of the Society for Research in Child Development Inc. Vol. XVII, Serial No. 54, No. 1 (1953).

18. FLINT, BETTY M. *The Security of Infants.* Toronto: University of Toronto Press, 1959.

19. ———— "Infant Studies." *Bull. Inst. Child Study.* XXVI: 2 (101) (1964), 2–6.

20. FOSS, B. M., ed. *Determinants of Infant Behaviour.* London: Methuen & Co. Ltd., 1959.

21. GOLDFARB, W. "Variations in Adjustment of Institutionally Reared Children." *Child Develpm.* XVII (1947), 449–457.

22. ———— "Emotional and Intellectual Consequences of Psychologic Deprivation in Infancy: A Revaluation." *Psychopathology of Childhood,* Hoch & Zerbin, ed. New York, London: Grune & Strattan, 1955, 105–12.

23. HARLOW, H. F. "Primary Affectional Pattern in Primates." *Amer. J. Orthopsychiat.* XXX (1960), 676.

24. ———— "The Development of Affectional Patterns in Infant Monkeys." *Determinants of Infant Behaviour,* B. M. Foss, ed. London: Methuen, 1961, 75–89.

25. JOSSELYN, IRENE M. "Treatment of the Emotionally Immature Child in an Institutional Framework." *Amer. J. Orthopsychiat.* XX (1950), 317–409.

26. KESSON, W. "Research in the Psychological Development of Infants: An Overview." *Merrill-Palmer Quart.* IX (1965), 83–94.

27. KILGOUR, MARY. "An Adoptive Child in his New Home." *Bull. Inst. Child Study* XXII: 4 (1960), 87.

28. ———— "On Placing Children from an Institution." *Bull. Inst. Child Study* XXVI: 2 (101) (1964), 7–12.

29. ———— "The Jones Family." Public Relations Committee, Catholic Children's Aid Society of Metropolitan Toronto, 1960.

30. KLOCKENBERG, G. "Studies on Maternal Deprivation in Infants' Homes." *Acta Pediatr.* XLV (1956), 1–12.

31. KIRKPATRICK, M. *Feeding the Pre-School Child.* Toronto: Copp Clark, 1963.

32. LAPPIN, B. *The Redeemed Children.* Toronto: University of Toronto Press, 1963.

33. LAURIE, REGINALD S. "Experience with Therapy of Psychosomatic Problems in Infants." *Psychopathology of Childhood.*

34. LEWIS, H. & NOLAN, BARNARD PACELLA, ed. *Modern Trends in Child Psychiatry.* New York: International Universities Press, 1946.

35. MURPHY, LOIS B. et. al. *The Widening World of Childhood.* Basic Books Publishing Co. Ltd., 1962.

36. MURPHY, LOIS B. "Problems in Recognizing Emotional Disturbance in Children." *J. Child Welfare Amer.* 10 (December, 1963).

37. PROVENCE, SALLY & LIPTON, ROSE. *Children in Institutions.* New York: International Universities Press, 1962.
38. RHEINGOLD, HARRIET. "The Modification of Social Responsiveness in Institutional Babies." Monograph of the Society for Research in Child Development Inc. XXI. Serial No. 63 (1956), 2.
39. RHEINGOLD, H. L. & BAYLEY, N. "The Later Effects of an Experimental Modification of Mothering." *Child Develpm.* XXX (1959), 363.
40. RIBBLE, MARGARET. "Infantile Experience in Relation to Personality Development." *Personality and the Behaviour Disorders,* Vol. II. J. M. V. Hunt, ed. New York: The Ronald Press Co., 1944.
41. ROUDINESCO, JENNY. "Severe Maternal Deprivation and Personality Development in Early Childhood." *Understanding the Child* XXI: 4 (1952).
42. TRASLER, G. *In Place of Parents.* London: Routledge & Kegan Paul, 1964.
43. TAYLOR, ANN. "Studying Institutional Children in Their Homes." *Bull. Inst. Child Study* XXVI: 2 (101) (1964), 13–17.
44. ———— "Institutional Children in Adoptive Homes: An Evaluation of Development." Unpublished article.
45. *Well Children.* Staff of the Institute of Child Study. Toronto: University of Toronto Press, 1956.
46. WORLD HEALTH ORGANIZATION. "Deprivation of Maternal Care: A Reassessment of its Effects." Geneva, 1962.
47. YARROW, L. J. "Maternal Deprivation: Toward an Empirical and Conceptual Re-Evaluation." *Psychol. Bull.* LVIII (1961), 459.
48. ———— "Separation from Parents During Early Infancy." *Child Development Review.*
49. ———— "Research Dimensions of Early Maternal Care." *Merrill-Palmer Quart.* IX: 2 (1963).